Psychic Voyages

Psychic Voyages

By the Editors of Time-Life Books

TIME-LIFE BOOKS, ALEXANDRIA, VIRGINIA

CONTENTS

Journeys of the Spirit

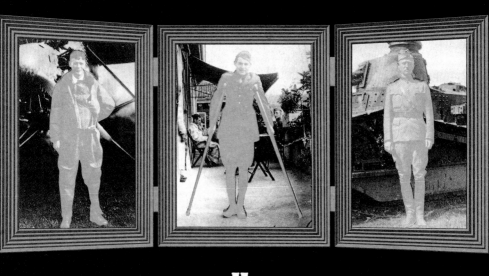

Human beings are limited by the physical world, by the capacities of the body and by the earthly laws of space and time. Understandably, then, an enduring belief held by humankind is that some part of us may be capable of breaking those bonds, that a spiritual or emotional essence can travel outside the body.

Underlying numerous philosophies and religions is the belief that the spirit and the body exist separately, and that the spirit or soul survives after death. But what of the spirit during life? Is it possible for a spiritual form to journey outside the physical body and then return? And if the spirit survives death, could it come back in another body? Throughout history, respected men and women have related their own experiences and answered yes.

These spiritual voyages are said to take one of three forms. During an out-of-body experience, the spirit travels beyond the physical body for a short time and then returns. In a near-death experience, the spirit departs as if bound for the next life but is drawn back into the still-living body. And spirits who appear to have survived the death of one physical body and then come back in another are said to have undergone reincarnation.

The prominent Americans pictured above each reported a type of spiritual travel. Details of aviator Charles A. Lindbergh's out-of-body experience, novelist Ernest Hemingway's near-death experience, and General George S. Patton's recollection of previous lives appear on the following pages.

The Ghostly Flight of Charles A. Lindbergh

For Charles A. Lindbergh, the most extraordinary moments of his 1927 transatlantic flight may have taken place during the trip's twenty-second hour. Enveloped in a dense fog, staring blankly at the instrument panel, battling an overwhelming desire to sleep, Lindbergh felt himself becoming as formless as a ghost.

"I existed independently of time and matter," he recalled nearly fifty years later. "I felt myself departing from my body as I imagine a spirit would depart—emanating into the cockpit, extending through the fuselage as though no frame or fabric walls were there, angling upward, outward, until I re-formed in an awareness far distant from the human form I left in a fast-flying transatlantic plane. But I remained connected to my body through a long-extended strand, a strand so tenuous that it could have been severed by a breath."

Lindbergh realized others would attribute his out-of-body experience to extreme fatigue; in his autobiography, the aviator responded to that logic. "My visions," he wrote, "are easily explained away through reason, but the longer I live, the more limited I believe rationality to be."

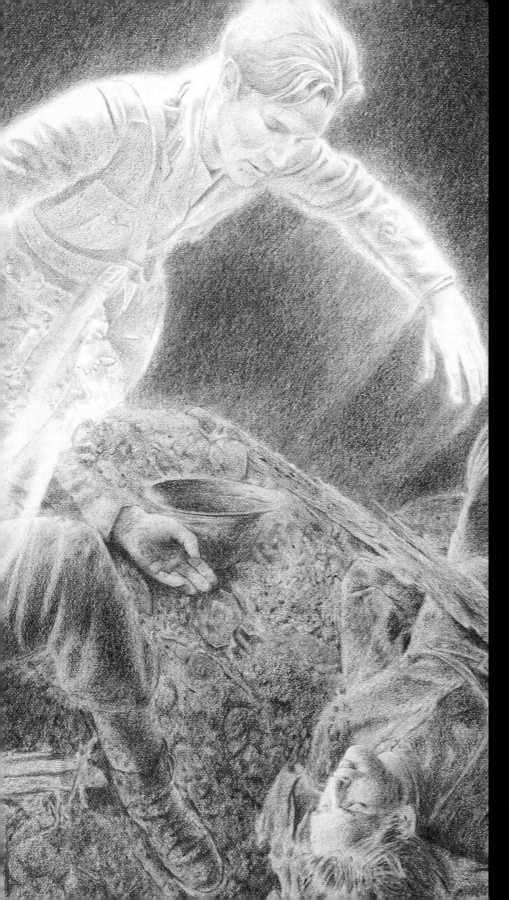

A Taste of Death for Ernest Hemingway

It was an oppressive ly hot July night in 1918. On the Italian front near the village of Fossalta, only the ligh from enemy fire illuminated the moonles sky. Crouched in a dugout, Ernest Heming way, a young officer with the U.S. Ambu lance Corps during World War I, listened in tently to the staccato of small-arms and mortar fire. Suddenly, he heard a morta shell hurtling through the air; an instant lat er, fire exploded around him and shrapnel splintered his legs. In the agonizing mo ments following the blast, Hemingway late told a friend, he sensed his spirit leaving hi body, as if in death.

Hemingway also described his own near death experience in his 1929 novel, *A Fare well to Arms,* in the episode in which the fic tional Frederic Henry is wounded. "I tried to breathe but my breath would not come," says Henry in the novel. "I felt myself rush bodily out of myself and out and out and ou and all the time bodily in the wind. I wen out swiftly, all of myself, and I knew I was dead and that it had all been a mistake to think you just died. Then I floated and in stead of going on I felt myself slide back. breathed and I was back."

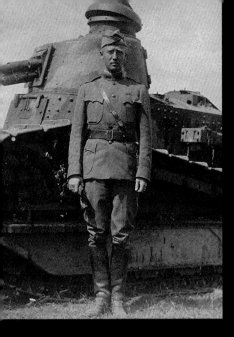

The Many Incarnations of George S. Patton

Captain George S. Patton had never before visited Langres, a small town in northeastern France. But in December 1917, having just arrived to operate a tank school, the American newcomer declined the offer of a local liaison officer to show him around the town, once the site of a Roman military camp. "You don't have to," Patton told the surprised young man. "I know it well."

A staunch believer in reincarnation, Patton felt sure that he had been to France before—as a Roman legionnaire. As he led the way through the area, he pointed out the sites of the ancient Roman temples and amphitheater, the drill ground, and the forum, even showing a spot where Julius Caesar had made his camp. It was, Patton later told his nephew, "as if someone were at my ear whispering the directions."

Patton may have credited his continuing military success, in part, to having been a soldier in other battles, in past lives. Once, in North Africa during World War II, a British general complimented Patton: "You would have made a great marshal for Napoleon if you'd lived in the eighteenth century." Patton merely grinned. "But I did," he replied.

CHAPTER 1

Leaving the Body Behind

One autumn evening in 1910, Caroline Larsen lay in bed in Burlington, Vermont, listening as her husband rehearsed a Beethoven string quartet downstairs with three other amateur musicians. She was drowsily enjoying the music when suddenly she was seized by a feeling of apprehension, as though she were about to faint.

"I braced myself against it, but to no avail," she related later. "The overpowering oppression deepened and soon numbness crept over me until every muscle became paralyzed . . . . At first I heard the music plainly . . . until finally everything became a blank . . . . The next thing I knew was that I, I myself, was standing on the floor beside my bed looking down attentively at my own physical body lying in it."

As Mrs. Larsen gazed down at her face, pale and still as death, the eyes closed and the mouth partly open, she felt no horror or shock but instead a calm sort of curiosity. She looked around the room; everything appeared to be in perfect order—the table with books and trinkets, the bureau, dresser, chairs, the green carpet and red wallpaper with its pattern of urns and flowers, figures that she had so often counted when she lay sleepless. She glanced once more at her body in the bed, then walked slowly out the door and down the hall to the bathroom, where there was a large mirror. "Through force of habit," she recalled, "I went through the motions of turning on the electric light, which of course I did not actually turn on." But there was no need: From her face and body emanated a strong whitish light that illuminated the room brilliantly.

"Looking into the mirror I became aware for the first time of the astonishing transformation I had undergone," she continued. "Instead of seeing a middle-aged woman, I beheld the figure of a girl about eighteen years of age. I recognized the form and features of my girlhood. But I was now infinitely more beautiful. My face appeared as if it were chiseled out of the finest alabaster and it seemed transparent, as did my arms and hands when I raised them to touch my hair . . . . But they were not entirely translucent, for in the center of the arms and hands and fingers there was a darker, more compact substance, as in X-ray photographs. My eyes, quite strong in the physical body, were piercingly keen now . . . . My hair, no longer grey, was now, as in my youth, dark brown and it fell in waves over my shoulders and down my back. And, to my delight, I was dressed in the loveliest white shining garment imaginable—a sleeveless one-piece dress, cut low at the neck and reaching almost to the ankles.''

Mrs. Larsen had lost track of the music while studying herself in the mirror. But now she heard the discordant strains of a Mendelssohn violin concerto being played badly. "I knew at once that the Frenchman was playing the solo," she recounted. "It was a habit he always indulged while the music was being changed on the stands. But, as always, he played it out of tune. As usual I felt disgusted and for the moment forgetting all about myself I muttered angrily 'Oh! I wish my husband would tell that Frenchman to play that concerto in tune or not to play it at all.' '' Fortunately, the quartet soon resumed its Beethoven. The music soothed Mrs. Larsen, and she was struck by a splendid idea. She would go downstairs and show off her youthful beauty before the men. How admiring they would be.

"Turning away from the mirror I walked out into the hall," she continued. "Enjoying in anticipation the success of my plan, I stepped on gaily. I reveled in the feeling of bodily lightness . . . . I moved with the freedom of thought." The music sounded lovelier than ever as Mrs. Larsen started down the stairs. But her hopes were soon dashed: "Just as I came to the little platform which divides the stairway into two flights, I saw, standing before me, a woman spirit in shining clothes with arms outstretched and with forefinger pointing upwards . . . . She spoke to me sternly, 'Where are you going? Go back to your

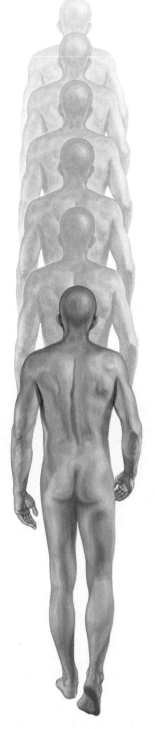

body!' . . . . I knew instinctively—that from this spirit's command and authority there was no appeal.''

Reluctantly heeding the command of the unknown spirit, Mrs. Larsen turned and ascended the stairs to her bedroom. "My physical body lay there," she said, "as still and lifeless as when I left it. I viewed it with feelings of loathing and disappointment. I knew that I would soon have to enter it again, no matter how ugly it seemed to me or how much I shrank from it." But there was no time for reflection. "In another instant I had again joined with my physical form. With a gasp and a start, I woke up in it.''

Caroline Larsen was by no means the first, and will certainly not be the last, person to feel the core of his or her self split off from the physical body. Such out-of-body experiences—or OBEs, as they are familiarly called—have been recorded since the beginnings of history by many people in all manner of cultures in every part of the world.

No particular ethnic group or nationality seems greatly more prone to OBEs than others. They occur among Tibetans as well as Icelanders; as commonly among the French as among Russians, Britons, and Americans; and they have been widely recorded among the primitive peoples of Borneo, Africa, and Oceania. Nor does any individual occupation appear to bring forth many more OBEs than another—though numerous creative writers claim to have undergone OBEs and have described them vividly. The German poet Goethe, for example, underwent a number of out-of-body experiences, as did D. H. Lawrence, Aldous Huxley, Arthur Koestler, Emily Brontë, Guy de Maupassant, and Jack London, to name only a few.

Yet for every well-known person who

has been involved in an OBE, there are thousands of ordinary men and women—like Caroline Larsen—who have felt themselves carried along on some sort of fantastic psychic voyage. Certain circumstances seem to favor OBEs: sleep and dreaming, hallucinogenic drugs and general anesthetics, and very serious illnesses or close encounters with death itself. People who have been on the brink of death or even clinically dead, only to return to life, often claim to have experienced a type of OBE that is referred to as a near-death experience, or NDE. And then there is reincarnation.

One might speculate, if the soul can voyage outside the body in life and survive death, then could it not be reborn in another body? The idea of reincarnation, as ancient as civilization, is being pursued by ardent researchers using the techniques of twentieth-century science. Indeed, the whole phenomenon of psychic voyages is today the subject of scientific scrutiny, though there are many members of the academic community who recoil at the very mention of the word science in connection with such things.

The critics dismiss psychic voyages—OBEs, NDEs, reincarnation, and the rest—as dreams or hallucinations or even fraud. Proponents, on the other hand, firmly hold that genuine out-of-body experiences entail a far greater sense of reality than has been demonstrated by ordinary dreams or hallucinations, both at the time of the experience and in retrospect. Moreover, say the advocates, the patterns of psychic mind-travel are all so amazingly similar and occur among so many completely unrelated people in such diverse places and walks of life that the phenomenon is unlikely to be the mere dreams or hallucinations of a relatively few susceptible people.

To the contrary, one student of OBEs, Dr. Eugene E. Barnard, has estimated that 1 out of every 100 people experiences an actual OBE at some time during his or her lifetime. Others suggest that the incidence might be as high as 15 or 20 percent.

Another psychic researcher, Dr. Charles T. Tart, has written: "Because of its apparently universal distribution across cultures and throughout history, out-of-the-body experiences constitute what the psychiatrist Carl Jung termed an 'archetypal' experience—an experience potentially available to many members of the human race simply by virtue of being human."

OBEs were frequently reported in ancient civilizations. The Egyptians believed that each individual possessed an astral, or spiritual, second body in the form of a bird with a human face; at death, this astral body, called *ba*, departed the physical body but hovered close to it. In sixth-century Greece, a mystic known as Hermotimus of Clazomene was said to travel widely in the spiritual realm, leaving his physical self behind in his wife's care. One day, weary of these lengthy absences, she asked two of Hermotimus's acquaintances to hide the body temporarily in hopes of scaring her husband into remaining at home. Unhappily, the two so-called friends secretly detested Hermotimus. They burned his body, leaving his soul to wander aimlessly forever.

In Old Testament times, the prophet Elisha was said to have exercised his out-of-body powers by voyaging through the air into the bedroom of a hostile Syrian king, there to eavesdrop on the king's military plans; thus did the Israelites thwart a Syrian attack on their homeland.

In the Christian era, the appearances of the resurrected Jesus are sometimes offered as evidence of out-of-body phenomena, and a number of Catholic saints have been said to travel out of their bodies. For example, the story is told of a day in the year 1226, when Saint Anthony of Padua was preaching in a church in Limoges, France; suddenly, the saint remem-

The ancient Egyptians thought of the astral body, or ba, as a birdlike spirit with a human head. In this painting from about 1250 B.C., the ba has left the physical body but hovers close above it.

bered that he was also supposed to be reading the scripture at a monastery some distance away in another part of Limoges. Saint Anthony quietly drew his hood over his head and knelt in silence for several minutes, while the church congregation waited in reverent patience. In those moments, the saint materialized among the monks at the monastery and read the appointed lesson. He then vanished. Meanwhile, at the church, Saint Anthony returned to his kneeling body and resumed his sermon.

Similar episodes were reported to involve Saint Severns of Ravenna, Saint Ambrose, and Saint Clement of Rome. And in 1774, Saint Alphonsus Liguori was said to have collapsed after celebrating Mass, remaining unconscious for twenty-four hours. Upon awakening, he related that he had been present at the deathbed of Pope Clement XIV in Rome. His news, and the exact time of the Pope's demise, were later confirmed by a papal envoy. Moreover, those present at the Pope's bedside stated that they had seen Alphonsus among the grieving company, praying for the dying pontiff.

As with churchmen, there was widespread agreement among early European peasants that the soul flew out of the body and traveled around freely during sleep. Such beliefs gave rise to the folklore of a body double that was something like the ancient Egyptian ba: It was known as *doppelganger* in German, *vardger* in Norwegian, *taslach* in Scottish, and *fetch* in Old English. Such beliefs persisted in the background of Western culture until the nineteenth century, when the entire range of similar phenomena became the focus of a broad popular interest in what was known as

Spiritualism, a religion that focused on communication with the deceased. The basic tenet of Spiritualism was that all people survive death as ghostly entities with special powers. In their new life, these entities evolve toward spiritual perfection in a world of inconceivable beauty and pleasure, and they can communicate their experiences to the living through mediums in séances.

Starting in the early 1850s, Spiritualism came to flower throughout the United States and Europe; at one point there were scores of mediums and 40,000 confirmed Spiritualists in New York City alone. In addition, many people embraced the idea of ghostly survival without formally becoming Spiritualists. But numerous frauds were exposed on both sides of the Atlantic, and responsible investigators quickly realized that they would have to subject the whole notion of spiritualism to serious, methodical scrutiny if they were to lend it credence. Thus, in 1882, a circle of eminent Victorians in and around Cambridge University founded the Society for Psychical Research, or SPR, "to investigate that large body of debatable phenomena designated by such terms as mesmeric, psychical and spiritualistic, without prejudice or prepossession of any kind, and in the same spirit of exact and unimpassioned enquiry which has en-

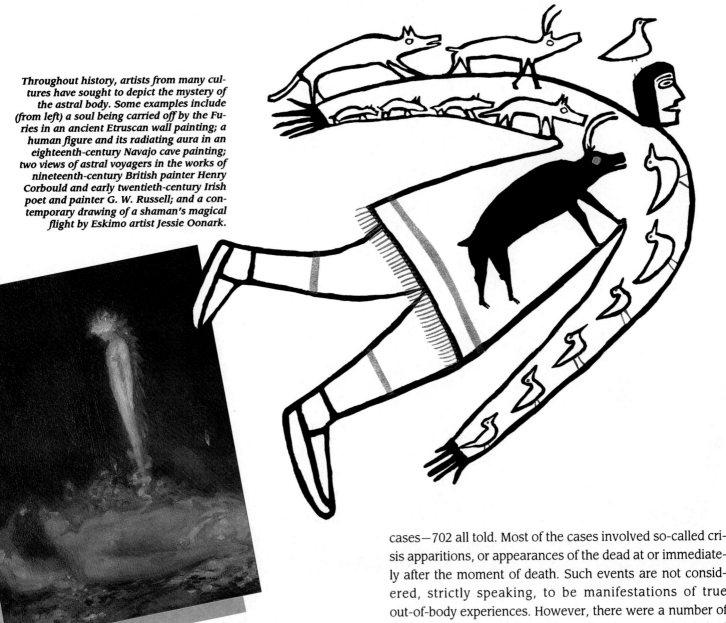

Throughout history, artists from many cultures have sought to depict the mystery of the astral body. Some examples include (from left) a soul being carried off by the Furies in an ancient Etruscan wall painting; a human figure and its radiating aura in an eighteenth-century Navajo cave painting; two views of astral voyagers in the works of nineteenth-century British painter Henry Corbould and early twentieth-century Irish poet and painter G. W. Russell; and a contemporary drawing of a shaman's magical flight by Eskimo artist Jessie Oonark.

abled science to solve so many problems." The SPR attracted some of the most notable personages of the day: Arthur Balfour, who would later become Britain's prime minister; the philosopher Henry Sidgwick; his wife, Eleanor, who had achieved the extraordinary distinction for a woman in that era of being named principal of one of the Cambridge colleges; and the notable physicist, Sir Oliver Lodge, who had embraced Spiritualism and sought to communicate with his dead son. Together they had the social and intellectual influence to carry out psychical research without serious concern for their reputations.

In 1886, SPR members Edmund Gurney, Frederic Myers, and Frank Podmore collaborated on *Phantasms of the Living,* a monumental two-volume tome that was three years in the making. It cataloged an enormous number of cases—702 all told. Most of the cases involved so-called crisis apparitions, or appearances of the dead at or immediately after the moment of death. Such events are not considered, strictly speaking, to be manifestations of true out-of-body experiences. However, there were a number of other occurrences in which apparitions of living people had reportedly been seen far from where their physical bodies were known to have been, and even cases where people claimed to have actually and purposely willed their discarnate selves to appear in the view of others.

In one such incident, a member of the society reported that he had once paid a visit in spirit form to the bedroom of two lady friends who lived three miles from his own house. Later, he said, he learned that his friends had been more than a little startled by the sight of him standing at their bedside in evening dress.

After due deliberation, the authors of *Phantasms* concluded that although it was quite common to receive a powerful mental impression of distant persons—perhaps through the supernatural power of telepathy, or mind reading—the actual persons had not truly traveled out-of-body. But others who had studied similar phenomena reached a

The eminent British physicist Sir Oliver Lodge—shown here with his secretary in 1936—was an early member of the Society for Psychical Research. His interests centered on the spiritual realm.

different conclusion; they firmly believed that out-of-body experiences did, in fact, occur.

The French researcher Adolphe d'Assier, for one, theorized that people's physical bodies contain doubles that are real, physical entities but composed of a more subtle matter than flesh. According to d'Assier, these doubles can depart the body, and they survive it in death. Eventually, a number of other researchers, among them Frederic Myers himself, became believers and concluded that there was overwhelming evidence for survival of the spirit after physical death. Myers wrote of it in *Human Personality and Its Survival of Bodily Death,* an enormous unfinished work published in 1903 after his own death. He also concluded

that "self-projection"—his term for astral travel—is "the one definite act which it seems as though a man might perform equally well before and after bodily death."

The explorations of the British SPR were augmented by those of its American counterpart, the American Society for Psychical Research, which was founded in 1885, three years after the original. Together the two societies gathered an astounding amount of anecdotal material supporting OBEs. Spiritualism offered ready explanations for these occurrences, which fit loosely within traditional Christian theology. But other enthusiasts in the late nineteenth and early twentieth centuries developed entirely new religious systems in order to explain them.

One of the most famous—and assuredly most controversial—of these systems was Theosophy. Its founder, Madame Helena Petrovna Blavatsky, was a Russian spiritualist who had wandered around the world and through a number of bigamous marriages before arriving destitute in New York in 1873. She found her life's calling through a chance meeting with Colonel Henry Olcott, a lawyer and journalist who was also a spiritualist. Olcott was greatly impressed with Madame Blavatsky's apparent powers; with his financial backing the two of them launched the Theosophical Society in 1875.

The term theosophy was taken from the Greek words for god and wisdom. The society would be composed, wrote Madame Blavatsky, "of learned occultists . . . and of passionate antiquaries and Egyptologists generally. We want to make an experimental comparison between Spiritualism and the magic of the ancients."

What followed was often a bit odd, even by the sometimes zany standards of the day's more ardent spiritualists. In one "experimental comparison," for example, a group of fervent Theosophists subjected a cat to a mild electrical shock. The cat rose some distance into the air, leading the experimenters to decide that levitation was electrical at its root; hoping to help the animal achieve total weightlessness, they increased the current. Sadly, they reported, "the poor cat suddenly expired."

The Theosophical Society attracted few followers in its first years. But in 1877, Madame Blavatsky published *Isis Unveiled,* a study of the occult inspired, it was claimed, by astral visions. Colonel Olcott reported, "Her pen would be flying . . . when she would suddenly stop, look into space with the vacant eye of the clairvoyant seer . . . and begin copying on her paper what she saw."

The book *Isis Unveiled* painted its author as a woman of tremendous learning, versed in a vast body of ancient spiritual truths. Disembodied spirits had been an integral part of the lost religions of antiquity, advised Madame Blavatsky, and these religions had involved much higher spiritual forms than those the "showmen" of modern times were producing at their séances. She suggested that she had access to these unseen but powerful beings and that she had been chosen by

them to mount a revival of primal truths in the modern world.

Among these alleged truths—and a central tenet of Theosophy—was that human beings exist on many planes besides the purely physical one. One of these levels is the astral body, a ghostly reproduction of the physical self that can travel far and wide outside the physical body. Everyone's astral body journeys during sleep, according to Madame Blavatsky, but the truly adept can will their astral bodies out of their physical selves by means of what she called astral projection. Moreover, those who are expert in the astral arts are able to see other people's astral bodies in plain daylight. They appear as multicolored halos around the physical body and reveal the essence of each personality through a range of colors.

The book achieved a modest success, and the society gained something of a following. Yet when hostile critics incessantly scoffed that it was all nonsense and published accusations of fraud along with unpleasant stories about Madame Blavatsky's background, she and the colonel decided to take the movement to India, where, as she put it, "no one will know my name."

For centuries, the pineal gland has been considered by some to be a third eye—the point where spirit and body join. In this 1962 interpretive painting of the head of Minerva, by Mihran K. Serailian, the pineal gland (shown at the center in deep blue)—radiates an aura that encompasses the pituitary gland (in red); the combined forces of these two glands are allegedly responsible for true spiritual illumination. During out-of-body travel, a silver cord emanating from near the third eye supposedly links the spiritual self to the body.

But once she was in India, the Blavatsky name was soon known well enough. So intriguing were her ideas and so hypnotic was her personality that Theosophy gained a considerable following among both Indians and British colonials. Much of Madame Blavatsky's renown was based on a series of allegedly miraculous phenomena, including a number of magically appearing letters that were, she said, "precipitated" by a race of immortals that lived in the Himalayas. Blavatsky claimed to be the pupil and devoted servant of these savants, who were known as Mahatmas, or Masters. Before long, her movement had spread back westward, with branches sprinkled throughout England, France, and other European countries. In the year 1884, Blavatsky and Olcott traveled to Europe to meet their new disciples; while they were there, they went before the Society for Psychical Research in order to present evidence of the marvels they had observed.

Whether favorably disposed or skeptical, the SPR dispatched Richard Hodgson to India to investigate the pair's claims. His report was devastating. He stated flatly that the so-called Mahatma letters were fraudulent, the result of some clever conjuring on the part of Madame Blavatsky. The lady, concluded Hodgson, could be described "neither as the mouthpiece of hidden seers, nor as a mere vulgar adventuress; we think she has achieved title to permanent remembrance as one of the most accomplished, ingenious and interesting impostors of history."

Undaunted by the appraisal of the Society for Psychical Research, Madame Blavatsky spent the better part of her remaining years in England, lecturing to her still loyal followers and writing constantly. In her last book, a major work entitled *The Secret Doctrine,* she laid out a complex occult system that involved, among many other things, a process of spiritual evolution through reincarnation.

Whether or not Madame Blavatsky was a charlatan, the essence of her system—that there was a psychic self which could travel outside the body—was remarkably consistent with the mass of OBE testimony. Whatever her faults, she provided welcome explanations to many psychic voyagers bewildered by their alleged experiences.

Most of those experiences appeared to be spontaneous, once-in-a-lifetime events. But there were a few individuals who claimed that they traveled out of their physical bodies on a regular basis and that they could evoke such experiences at will.

The first such frequent out-of-body voyager in recent history was an Englishman named Hugh G. Calloway, who would later chronicle his OBE exploits under the pseudonym of Oliver Fox. Born in 1885, he was a sickly, high-strung child going from one illness to another—"It's the croup again," were the first words he recalled having heard—and prone as well to intense dreams and nightmares. Calloway was very young when he began to develop his apparent psychic powers. His dreams always started the same way, with small blue or mauve vibrating circles "resembling a mass of frogs' eggs," as he put it. Then the circles would turn into either small glass inkpots, in which case the night would pass relatively peacefully, or tiny grinning faces with piercing blue eyes, in which case the child would suffer a nasty nightmare. "Thereafter, I performed a feat of childish magic," said Calloway. "When the empty circles came I would give the command, 'Let it be inkstands!' for I confused the pot with the stand in those days. Sure enough, the little glass pots would appear and there would be no nightmare. But I had to be very quick or the grinning faces would get in first."

When Calloway was thirteen, he lost his mother, and his father followed her to the grave within six months. The youth, who had always feared death, then underwent a change of attitude and turned inward. "Beyond the grave, I should surely meet my mother," he remembered musing, "and that thought robbed the mysterious next world of most of its terrors and greatly stimulated my interest in the after-life. Beautiful Mother, big omniscient Daddy—where were they now?"

As he grew more mature, Hugh Calloway's dreams became more vivid and complex. "Most of them were obvi-

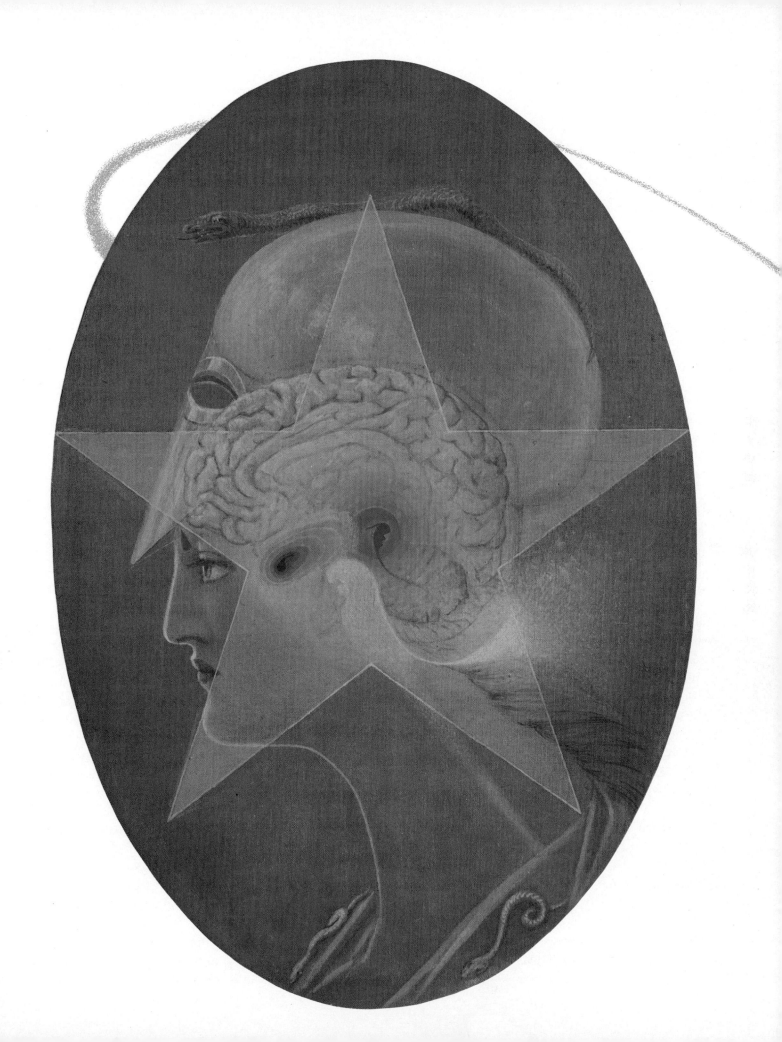

ously a more or less nonsensical mix-up," he recalled. Now and then, however, he would have prophetic dreams, but these involved only trivial things. On occasion, he would also have historical dreams, set on a grand scale, dreams in which he was not a participant but a spectator. And when he dreamed of his mother, the visions "were so charged with her fragrant atmosphere that on waking it seemed as if I had only just left her presence."

Calloway also began to have what he termed "dreams of knowledge," in which he actually understood that he was dreaming. One night at Southampton University, where he was studying electrical engineering, he dreamed that he was standing on the pavement outside his dormitory. His impressions were strong, and he was sure that he was awake, until he noticed that the stones in the pavement, which in reality were laid perpendicular to the curb, were now placed parallel to it. Instantly, he realized that he was dreaming, and the realization filled him with an exquisite sense of freedom and power.

Calloway claimed that he went on to experience many of these so-called dreams of knowledge, in which the realization that he was dreaming allowed him freedom of action in them. He could command himself to rise off the ground, glide at a height of 100 feet, and pass through walls, although he was always eventually called back to his body by some unknown force that made his head ache when he attempted to resist it.

One night, Calloway finally defied that force by willing himself to remain in a dream until, with a curious click, the pain vanished, and he knew that he was at last entirely free of his physical self. The trouble came, he related, when he tried to get back into his body and could not. With a mighty effort, he finally willed himself back, only to discover to his horror that he could not move a muscle. Finally, by concentrating on raising a single finger, he managed to overcome the paralysis, queasy but determined to continue what he called his "experiments."

To be sure, the vast majority of Calloway's experiences were impossible to verify, since they were based solely on his own testimony. But he did report several occurrences involving other psychic travelers, who in turn testified that their experiences coincided with his. Two of his college friends shared his interest in such matters, and one night the trio decided to meet out-of-body on the university commons; Calloway and one of his friends made the psychic rendezvous, both dreaming that they had met the other at the appointed place that night.

On another occasion, one of Calloway's early sweethearts, named Elsie, reportedly came to his room as an apparition the night after he had chastised her for doubting the reality of his journeys. Calloway had called her a "narrow-minded little ignoramus," and so the young lady determined to show him who the real ignoramus was. That night Calloway saw in his bedroom a large egg-shaped cloud of intense bluish-white light, in the center of which stood Elsie, in a nightgown and with her hair loose. "She seemed perfectly solid as she stood by a chest of drawers near the right side of my bed," said Calloway. "Thus she remained, regarding me with calm but sorrowful eyes, and running her fingers along the top and front side of a desk which stood on the drawers."

Calloway could neither move nor utter a word; that same paralysis he had experienced previously had set in. "At last, I broke the spell," recounted Calloway. "Rising on one elbow, I called her name, and she vanished as suddenly as she had come."

The following evening, by Calloway's account, he met Elsie, and she exclaimed, "I did come to you. I really did. I went to sleep, willing that I would, and all at once I was there. This morning I knew just how everything was in your room." And Elsie, who had never seen Calloway's room nor discussed its layout, proceeded to describe it all in perfect detail, including the fact that Calloway had been lying, eyes open, on the left side of a double bed and seemed dazed.

"I have never ceased being grateful to dear Elsie for being 'wicked' just for once," wrote Calloway. "Truth to tell, though a few of my friends were sympathetic, the world refused to be impressed by my great discovery . . . . When I tried to get into print, one editor actually insinuated in polite-nasty fashion that mouse-like flying quadripeds inhabited my campanile."

Bats in his belfry or not, Calloway continued his investigations and adopted Madame Blavatsky's Theosophy as his theoretical model. Like the Theosophists, he believed that most of his travels took place in the astral plane through the vehicle of his astral body. He claimed to have learned the technique of "skrying," or rising through the higher planes of existence, but was frightened by one trip that seemed to take him to the edge of outer space, where he encountered an awe-inspiring succession of concentric circles of light. Calloway also reported that he had learned how to induce a trance without falling asleep and that he had eventually perfected a way of leaving his body through what he called his pineal door. (The pineal gland, located deep within the brain and thought by some to be the seat of the soul, has long been regarded as the organic component of out-of-body experiences.)

Calloway's psychic travels took him farther and farther afield. Once, he wrote, he found himself in the middle of a glittering oriental city with ornate bazaars and an immense sculptured black elephant in a kneeling position. On another occasion, while he was attempting an ambitious out-of-body journey to a Tibetan temple, he fell into what first seemed to be an endless darkness and silence until he discovered himself in a terrifying torture chamber, bound naked to a rack and bleeding from wounds and burns inflicted by robed interrogators who were trying to force him to renounce his true identity. He refused, and was immediately cast back to waking life in his physical body.

In recording his experiences, Calloway suggested several methods for achieving OBEs, including how to make a dream of knowledge ("send the body to sleep while the mind is kept awake") and how to pass through the pineal door ("concentrate upon an imaginary trap-door within the brain"). He hastened to add, however, that OBEs were not for everybody: "No one with a weak heart should seek prac-

tical acquaintance with the phenomenon of separation; and very excitable, nervous people would do well to leave the subject alone."

During the 1920s, Calloway wrote accounts of his OBEs for a British psychical journal; in 1938, using his Oliver Fox pseudonym, he published his experiences in book form. By then, however, his work in the field had been all but eclipsed by the testimony of a young American named Sylvan Joseph Muldoon.

Born in about 1903, Muldoon was an avid student of the occult. In 1927, he read in a book by the noted British-born psychical researcher Hereward Carrington that a Frenchman named Charles Lancelin had written nearly all that was known about the subject of astral projection. Muldoon quickly fired off a letter to Carrington, informing him that he, Muldoon, could fill a book with material unknown to Lancelin. Intrigued, Carrington was soon collaborating with Muldoon on a book about the young man's experiences entitled *The Projection of the Astral Body*. Published in 1929, the book caused a mild sensation among the relatively small coterie of OBE enthusiasts.

By Muldoon's account, his introduction to out-of-body experiences had occurred when he was twelve years old. His mother, who was an active spiritualist, had taken her young son with her to a Spiritualist Association camp in Clinton, Iowa. In the dead of his first night there, Muldoon awoke with a start. "I was powerless," he recalled. "My entire rigid body (I thought it was my physical, but it was my astral) commenced vibrating at a great rate of speed, in an up-and-down direction, and I could feel a tremendous pressure being exerted in the back of my head . . . . Then the sense of hearing began to function, and that of sight followed. When able to see, I was more than astonished: I was floating in the air, rigidly horizontal a few feet above the bed . . . . Involuntarily, at about six feet above the bed . . . I was uprighted and placed standing upon the floor of the room . . . . Then I managed to turn around. There was another 'me' lying quietly on the bed. My two identical bodies were joined by means of an elastic-like cable which extend-

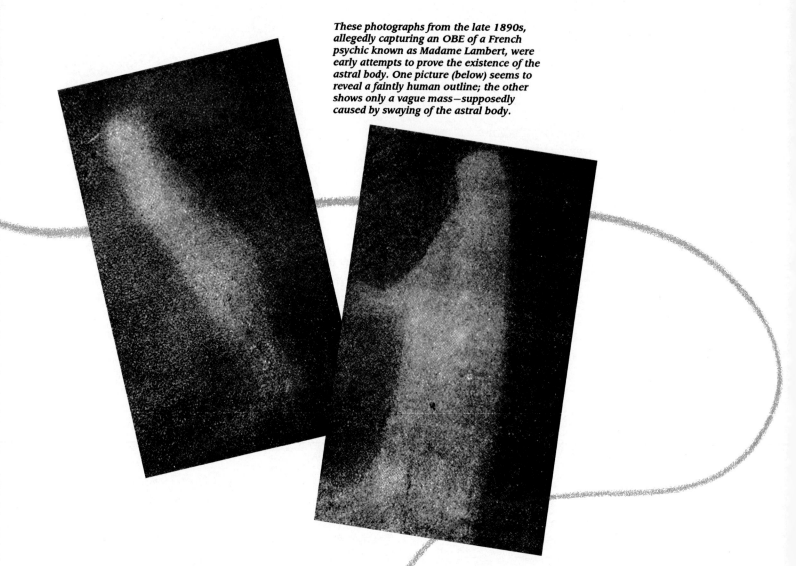

These photographs from the late 1890s, allegedly capturing an OBE of a French psychic known as Madame Lambert, were early attempts to prove the existence of the astral body. One picture (below) seems to reveal a faintly human outline; the other shows only a vague mass—supposedly caused by swaying of the astral body.

ed across the space of probably six feet which separated us .... My first thought was that I had died during sleep."

The disembodied Muldoon drifted into the room where his mother was sleeping and tried to shake her awake. But his hands passed right through her—and through the bodies of other people he attempted to rouse. The child began weeping and wandered around for another quarter of a hour until he was pulled back into his body by his cable, or cord. "At the moment of coincidence," he later wrote. "every muscle in the physical body jerked, and a penetrating pain, as if I had been split open from head to foot, shot through me. I was physically alive again, as amazed as fearful. I had been conscious throughout the entire occurrence."

After recovering from his initial shock, Muldoon went on to experience literally hundreds of projections, he said. The most remarkable took place in 1924, when he was twenty-one. He had gone out for a walk after supper, feeling listless and lonely, and had soon returned home, where he went to his room, locked the door, and threw himself on his bed. Soon his body began to turn numb, and he knew that a projection was coming on.

Moments later he felt his body rise up, at first horizontally off the bed, then rotate into a vertical position, which enabled him to move around freely. After he roamed through his house for a bit, he went outside and was suddenly carried away at fantastic speed to a strange place, a farmhouse, where he found four people together in a room. One of them was a pretty young girl of about seventeen; she was sewing something and Muldoon saw that it was a black dress. He moved forward until he was directly in front of the girl. He watched her sew for a short while, then went around the room looking at the furnishings. At that point, it occurred to Muldoon that he had no legitimate reason to be there, so he took one last glance around and left, shortly afterward reentering his body back home.

Some weeks later, according to Muldoon, he encountered the girl of his projection. He asked her where she lived, and she quite properly told him that it was none of his business. Whereupon young Muldoon described her home in precise detail, both outside and in. What the young lady said to that was not recorded. At any rate, she and Muldoon became fast friends, and he visited her home, which was fifteen miles away, a number of times; and Muldoon claimed that he recognized everything he had seen on his astral excursion.

Whereas Calloway advised caution, Muldoon in his writings urged readers to attempt out-of-body travel. His suggested techniques for inducing OBEs included trying to be fully conscious at the moment of falling asleep and seeking to invoke a dream that involved rising, flying, or ascending in an elevator. Muldoon also believed that most people experience subtle OBEs without ever realizing it: Actions like fainting or twitching when on the verge of sleep he regarded as examples of partial separation of the double from the body.

Muldoon and Carrington later collaborated on another book that explored numerous OBEs and many aspects of projection, and their works were probably the most widely read of the field's literature through World War II. Since that time, the best known of the putative astral travelers has been Robert Monroe, a former advertising executive who claims to have experienced his first out-of-body experience in 1958, at the relatively advanced age of forty-three. In every respect, Monroe was a perfectly normal and unexceptional American businessman: college educated and married, with children, a level-headed man with no serious vices or peculiarities. His only "unorthodox activity," as he put it, was "my experimentation with techniques of data learning during sleep—with myself as the chief subject."

Monroe suspects that these learning experiments—which involved listening to audiotapes while he slept—might have had something to do with his first OBEs. His first inkling that something unusual was happening came one Sunday after brunch, when he was seized by what he described as "a severe, iron-hard cramp, which extended across my diaphragm or solar plexus area just under my rib cage. It was a solid band of unyielding ache." Monroe thought it might be food poisoning, but none of the other family members felt ill. The cramp lasted from 1:30 in the afternoon until about midnight, when Monroe fell asleep from pure exhaustion. It was gone the next morning, and except for some soreness, there were no aftereffects. "In retrospect," said Monroe wryly, "perhaps it was the touch of a magic wand—or a sledge hammer."

Three weeks later, according to Monroe, again on a Sunday afternoon, he experienced another touch of that magic wand—or whatever it was. He was reclining comfortably when a ray, a beam of some sort, seemed to come out of the sky and strike his body, causing it to vibrate violently. "I was utterly powerless to move," reported Monroe of the incident. "It was as if I were being held in a vise." The vibration lasted only a few seconds, then faded.

Nine times during the next six weeks the same vibration returned—always when Monroe was lying down to rest or sleep—and faded away when he fought himself to a sitting position. On one occasion, he claimed, the vibrations developed into a ring of sparks, with Monroe's body being the axis in the center of the ring. "The ring would start at the head and slowly sweep down to my toes and back to the head, keeping this up in regular oscillation," said Monroe. "When the ring passed over my head, a great roaring surged with it, and I felt the vibrations in my brain."

Monroe anxiously consulted his family doctor, who assured him that he was not entering the first stages of schizophrenia. On the chance that some physical ailment might be at the root of his singular symptoms, Monroe underwent a thorough medical examination; he was not an epileptic, showed no signs of brain tumor, and was in fact perfectly healthy. The doctor suggested that he ease off working so hard, get more sleep, and lose some weight.

The vibrations continued. One night, as Monroe lay in bed, waiting for them to pass, his arm brushed the floor, and he pressed his fingers against the rug. They went right through to the floor; Monroe pushed harder and his fingers penetrated the floor to the area below, where he felt a small chip of wood, a bent nail, and some sawdust. Next, Monroe found that his whole arm was through the floor and that he was splashing his hand in water.

To put it mildly, Monroe was perplexed. "I was wide awake," he would recall. "I could see the moon-lit landscape through the window. I could feel myself lying on the bed, the covers over my body, the pillow under my head, my chest rising and falling as I breathed. The vibrations were still present, but to a lesser degree." Monroe wondered in awe, "How could I be awake in all other respects and still 'dream' that my arm was stuck down through the floor?"

Monroe mentioned his experience to a psychologist friend, who agreed that it was a pretty convincing daydream—if that was what it was. Half jokingly, he suggested that Monroe cut a hole in the floor to find out what was down there.

About a month later, the vibrations came again, and after a moment, Mon–

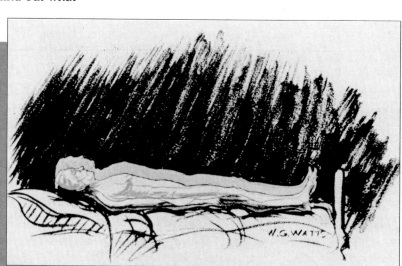

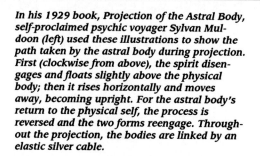

In his 1929 book, Projection of the Astral Body, self-proclaimed psychic voyager Sylvan Muldoon (left) used these illustrations to show the path taken by the astral body during projection. First (clockwise from above), the spirit disengages and floats slightly above the physical body; then it rises horizontally and moves away, becoming upright. For the astral body's return to the physical self, the process is reversed and the two forms reengage. Throughout the projection, the bodies are linked by an elastic silver cable.

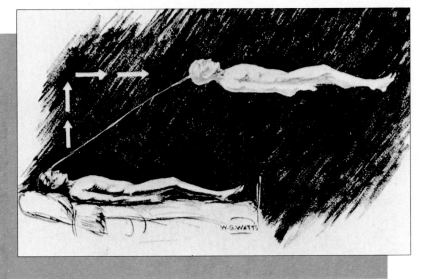

roe became aware of something pressing against his shoulder; it was smooth and he thought that it was the wall. But as he looked around him, he realized that it had no windows, no furniture against it, no doors. "It was the ceiling," said Monroe. "I was floating against the ceiling, bouncing gently with any movement I made. I rolled in the air, startled, and looked down. There, in the dim light below me, was the bed. There were two figures lying in the bed. To the right was my wife. Beside her was someone else . . . . I looked more closely, and the shock was intense. I was the someone on the bed!"

Monroe was stunned. "Here I was, there was my body. I was dying, this was death and I wasn't ready to die. Desperately, like a diver, I swooped down to my body and dove in. I then felt the bed and the covers, and when I opened my eyes, I was looking at the room from the perspective of my bed."

The next time he saw his psychologist friend, a concerned Monroe told him about his latest experience and said that he was not ready to die. "Oh, I don't think you'll do that," the psychologist reassured him calmly. "Some of the fellows who practice yoga and those Eastern religions claim that they can do it whenever they want." "Do what?" inquired Monroe. "Why, get out of their physical body for a while," the doctor replied. "They claim they can go all over the place. You ought to try it."

Indeed. In the years to come, Monroe would dedicate himself to exploring OBEs as thoroughly and systematically as he could. He kept detailed records of his alleged journeys, complete with verifiable information—insofar as that was possible—about the places he had visited.

Monroe claimed to have traveled in three different dimensions, which he designated as Locales I, II, and III. Locale I was the world as everyone knows it, and Monroe's travels usually took him to relatively familiar places close to home. Locale II was a different story altogether.

Monroe had some difficulty describing it, and chose his words carefully. He began by stating,

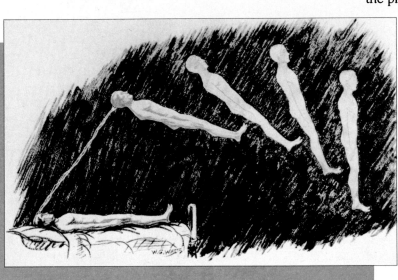

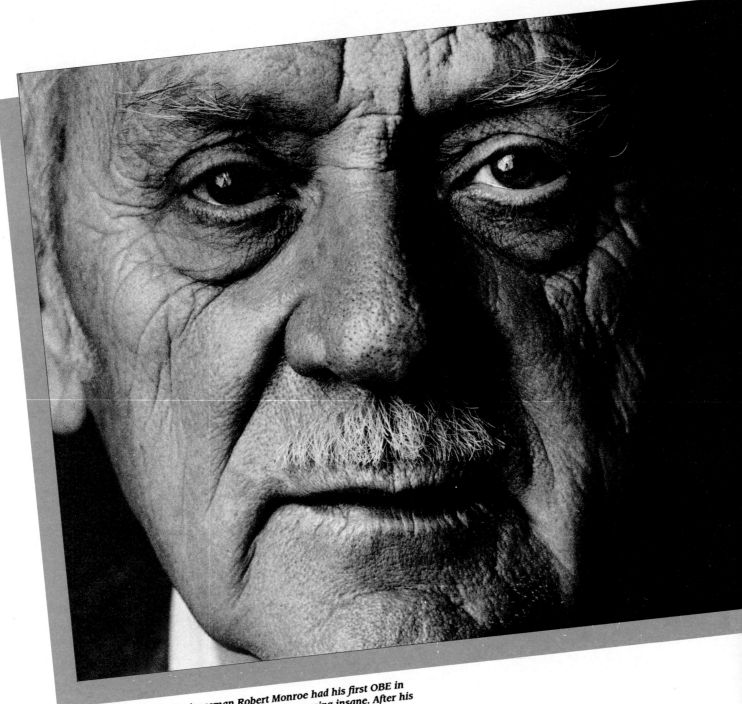

When middle-aged businessman Robert Monroe had his first OBE in 1958, he thought he might be hallucinating or going insane. After his initial shock, however, Monroe began to explore his newfound abilities and delighted in his discoveries. He kept meticulous records of his experiences and participated in laboratory experiments to discover more about the phenomenon. In 1971, Monroe published *Journeys Out of the Body*, a first-person account that chronicled his alleged astral travels to other dimensions and explained his techniques for inducing an OBE (opposite page).

"The best introduction to Locale II is to suggest a room with a sign over the door saying, 'Please Check All Physical Concepts Here.'" He went on to describe its immensity: "Locale II is a non-material environment with laws of motion and matter only remotely related to the physical world. It . . . has depth and dimensions incomprehensible to the finite, conscious mind. In this vastness lie all of the aspects we attribute to heaven and hell, which are but part of Locale II. It is inhabited, if that is the word, by entities with various degrees of intelligence with whom communication is possible."

Monroe continued. "Superseding all appears to be one prime law. Locale II is a state of being where that which we label thought is the wellspring of existence. It is the vital creative force that produces energy, assembles 'matter' into form, and provides channels of perception and communication . . . . In this environment, no mechanical supplements are found . . . . You *think* movement and it is fact."

Locale III, which Monroe supposedly visited a number of times on what he called "intrusions," seemed almost mundane in comparison with the others. This third dimension was, said Monroe, "a physical-matter world almost identical to our own. There are trees, houses, cities, people, artifacts and all the appurtenances of a reasonably civilized society." However, Monroe noted, Locale III had evolved on a somewhat different technological basis; there was no electricity or fossil fuels; its inhabitants relied instead on a sort of nuclear power.

And here, said Monroe, his disembodied double "met and 'merged' temporarily and involuntarily with one who can only be described as the 'I' who lives 'there.' I, fully conscious of living and being 'here,' was attracted to and began momentarily to inhabit the body of a person 'there,'

Monroe's Tips for Astral Travelers

According to Robert Monroe, anyone can travel outside the body—all it takes is practice and the desire to do it. For those attempting OBEs, Monroe suggests the following guidelines:

1. In a warm, dark room where you will not be disturbed, lie in a comfortable position with your head pointing north. Loosen clothes and remove any jewelry.

2. Relax your mind and body. Close your eyes and breathe rhythmically, keeping your mouth slightly open.

3. Focus on a single image as you drift toward sleep. When you reach the state bordering wakefulness and sleep, deepen your relaxation by concentrating on the blackness beyond your eyelids.

4. To induce the vibrations that allegedly herald the onset of an OBE, focus on a point about twelve inches from your forehead. Gradually extend the point of focus to a distance of six feet, and draw an imaginary line parallel to your body. Focusing on that plane, imagine the vibrations and bring them down into your head.

5. Gain control of the vibrations by consciously guiding them through your body—from your head to your toes and back again. Once these vibratory waves can be produced on mental command, you are ready to attempt separation from the body.

6. To leave the body, concentrate on how pleasant it would be to float upward. Maintain these thoughts, and your astral form should begin to rise.

7. To return to the physical self, simply focus on reengaging the two entities.

much like myself." Monroe's counterpart in Locale III— Monroe called him his "I" There—was an architect who lived in a boarding house and rode a bus to work; reasonably well-educated, he was a rather introspective person, and not notably prosperous. Monroe's adventures in Locale III included his counterpart's eventual marriage to Lea, a rich but depressed young woman with two children from a previous marriage. The union was not very successful, and they separated. Monroe's "I" There was unhappy over the alienation and promised to visit Lea, but he somehow lost the address. Shortly thereafter, Monroe's "intrusions" into the world of Locale III ceased.

What did Monroe make of all this? In view of the less-than-idyllic circumstances, he thought it unlikely to be an escape from reality via the unconscious. "One can only speculate," he said, "and such speculation of itself must consider concepts unacceptable to present-day science." Far different from the here and now of Locale I, Locale III was "neither the known past nor the present, and not the probable future." Monroe thought that "it might be a memory, racial or otherwise, of a physical earth civilization that predates known history. It might be another earth-type world located in another part of the universe which is somehow accessible through mental manipulation. It might be an antimatter duplicate of this physical earth-world where we are the same but different, bonded together unit for unit by a force beyond our present comprehension."

As enchanted as Monroe was with the wonders of his psychic voyages, he was also exceedingly meticulous in analyzing them. In his 1971 book, *Journeys Out of the Body,* he recorded every last detail and even subjected his travels to exhaustive statistical analysis. "Physical conditions" were usually warm (96.2%) and about evenly divided between day (42.2%) and night (57.8%); he was always prone (100%) and usually facing in a north-south direction (62.4%). Humidity and barometric pressure had no discernible effect. Monroe went on to quantify and tabulate, in numbing detail, statistics on such things as his tiredness level, psycho-

logical state, and eating habits as they related to his achievement of OBEs. Through it all, he was seeking insight into his psychic voyages—and undoubtedly striving to give his studies the appearance of scientific inquiry.

In the 1970s, Monroe made OBEs and other parapsychological phenomena his full-time occupation. He founded the Monroe Institute for Applied Sciences in rural Virginia to teach techniques for achieving OBEs and other altered states of consciousness. Monroe had induced his own early OBEs with techniques much like those of Calloway and Muldoon. But for OBE beginners at the institute, he created "hemi-sync" audiotapes, which combined various sounds with vocal instructions. Designed, said Monroe, to synchronize the electrical impulses of the right and left brain hemispheres, and thus enable listeners to explore their inner selves without encountering resistance from the brain, hemi-sync produced some interesting changes in perspective, if not actual out-of-body experiences in every case. Some versions of the tapes, in fact, were specially tailored to do such things as relieve insomnia and improve tennis and golf scores.

To be sure, Monroe is not without his detractors. One investigator who sought to verify Monroe's out-of-body visits to friends found no one who could corroborate his claims. Another has accused him of exaggerating and romanticizing his OBE accounts. Nevertheless, in 1982, the Monroe Institute, in conjunction with the University of Kansas Medical Center, was invited to present three papers on out-of-body experiences at a meeting of the American Psychiatric Association. Even at the scheduled early hour of 8:00 A.M., the papers were presented to a full house of more than 100 interested attendees.

Monroe contended that his appearance before the assembled psychiatrists somehow validated the whole notion of astral travel. "For them even to schedule and permit such papers to be read," he averred, "was an acknowledgment that such phenomena do exist." In fact, whatever goes on in the mind is of interest to medicine, and OBEs are nothing if not altered states of mind. Just how far they go beyond the realm of dreams and hallucinations remains the issue confronting researchers who seek answers in the testimony of alleged astral travelers.

Perhaps the most notable aspects of the three virtuosi of psychic voyaging—Calloway, Muldoon, and Monroe—are the common elements of their reports. For example, like many who have experienced spontaneous OBEs, all three were at one time or another aware of being attached to their physical bodies by means of a mysterious cord. Usually called "the silver cord," it is also known as Saint Paul's Cord because it was he, in I Corinthians, who long ago postulated the existence of a spiritual body linked to the physical body. The cord is said by believers to act as a sort of umbilical cord; so long as it remains intact, the psychic traveler is safe, but if it breaks, separation from the physical body is permanent, followed by death.

Muldoon's impression was of a silver-colored cable with a circumference about that of a silver dollar when the double was near the body; the cable could stretch to gossamer thinness when the voyager traveled far from the physical body. Calloway never actually saw his cord, but he claimed that on several occasions he felt something like a cord or a force tugging him back to physical reality.

Monroe never saw his cord either, but once when he reached behind himself, he said, he felt what could have been one coming out from between his shoulder blades. "It was hanging loosely," he recalled, "and I could feel its texture very definitely. It was body-warm to the touch and seemed to be composed of hundreds of tendon-like strands packed neatly together."

Yet for all their earnest studies and writings, Calloway, Muldoon, Monroe, and a few other deeply involved voyagers had until somewhat recently remained more or less alone in their efforts to validate OBEs. As widespread as the phenomenon seemed to be, there were few outside attempts to cast a cool scientific eye on out-of-body experiences until the 1960s, when Celia Green and Robert Crookall, two reputable British scientists, drew attention to such

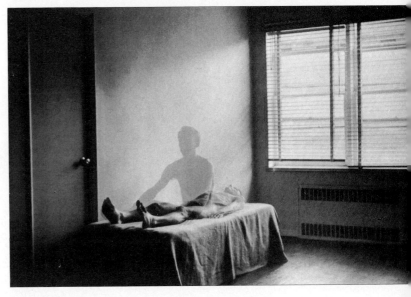

The realistic images shown here and on the next two pages are part of New York photographer Duane Michals's 1968 series depicting an OBE. Titled Spirit Leaving the Body, the series was inspired by the photographer's deep interest in astral travel; after studying the subject for a number of years, Michals recorded his interpretation of how the spiritual form is freed from the body.

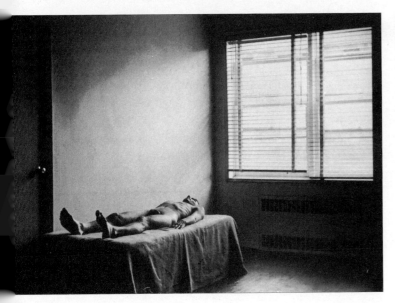

experiences through extensive surveys and case histories.

In 1961, Green founded the Institute of Psychophysical Research at Oxford and sent out an appeal through the press and radio, requesting details from persons who had undergone OBEs. In all, 326 people responded. Sixty of them had experienced only one OBE, twenty-one had had six or more, and eighteen had had between one and five. The group included people of all ages. Among those who had had more than one experience, the OBEs had started in childhood. Those who had undergone only a single OBE tended to have had the experience between the ages of 15 and 35. As a rule, the incidence of out-of-body journeys diminished with age.

Most of the cases were nowhere near as intense or

detailed as the experiences recounted by Monroe and the other famed voyagers; in fact, eighty of the group members reported no awareness of being in a second body but simply of being a "disembodied consciousness" somewhat removed from their physical body.

Green and others regarded it as significant that although only a few people may make prolonged and intense out-of-body journeys, many others may have had some sort of relevant experience at a lower level. Green reported one such brief excursion related by a young motorcyclist: "During the morning while driving fast along a road, the drone of the engine and vibration seemed to lull me into a stupor, and I remember I seemed to leave my motorbike like a zoom lens in reverse and was hovering over a hill watching myself and friend tearing along on the road below, and I seemed to think 'I shouldn't be here, get back on that bike!' and the next instant, I was in the saddle again."

Another example concerns a waitress who, after working a twelve-hour day, left the restaurant to walk home. "I remember feeling so fatigued that I wondered if I'd make it," she reported. "The next I registered was of hear-

ing the sound of my heels very hollowly and I looked down and watched myself walk round the bend of the street . . . . I saw myself very clearly—it was a summer evening and I was wearing a sleeveless shantung dress. I remember thinking 'so that's how I look to other people.' "

These and other cases like them suggest just a slightly altered state of consciousness, brought on in the one case by monotony and in the other by fatigue, but nevertheless a seemingly total awareness of a second self.

Crookall, who served as principal geologist at England's prestigious Institute of Geological Sciences, had a long-standing fascination with psychic phenomena. Following the examples of Carrington, Muldoon, and others, he collected and analyzed accounts of OBEs from people all over the world—close to a thousand in all—which he documented in several books. According to Crookall's analysis, most OBEs are marked by several common factors. The separation of the supposed astral body from its physical form, for instance, frequently begins at the hands and feet and ends at the head. Many out-of-body travelers report that they black out or hear clicking sounds at the moment of complete separation, but most claim that they feel no fear or discomfort.

The extensive material gathered by Green and Crookall convinced other investigators that documenting OBEs in a controlled laboratory environment was worth trying. The pioneer in such work was Dr. Charles T. Tart. In 1965 and 1966, while he was an instructor at the University of Virgin-

ia School of Medicine, Tart began a series of fascinating experiments with a subject called Mr. X, who lived near Charlottesville, where the university is located. Only later did it come out that Mr. X was in reality none other than Robert Monroe; if anybody had a good chance of calling up an out-of-body experience, he did.

Tart placed Monroe in a special room, where he was connected to machines that would monitor his heartbeat, brain waves, and rapid eye movements (or REMs, which indicate dream periods during sleep). Tart asked Monroe to induce an OBE and then project himself into an adjoining room. Once inside the room, Monroe was to read a randomly selected five-digit number on a shelf that was placed high enough to ensure that he could not see the number by normal vision.

Monroe, uncomfortable on an army cot with electrodes clamped to his head, was unsuccessful in his first seven attempts to induce an OBE in the laboratory. But in his eighth—and final—attempt, he reportedly felt his nonphysical body roll off the cot, float to the floor, and slowly drift through the door into the control room. He did not see the target numbers, but he did notice that the laboratory technician who should have been in the room was absent. He then floated into the brightly lit outer corridor, where he found the technician talking with a man who was unfamiliar to Monroe. Afterward, he related the experience to the technician, who confirmed that she had been in the corridor with her husband.

Tart deemed the Monroe series inconclusive but was determined to continue this line of research. After accepting a position at the University of California at Davis as a professor of psychology, he found a new subject—a bright college student he identified as Miss Z. She claimed to have experienced OBEs two to four times a week for most of her life, usually awakening during the night to find herself floating near the ceiling. As a child she had assumed that this was perfectly normal. Only as a teenager, when she began to describe these experiences to her friends, did she realize the extraordinary nature of her out-of-body travel.

By the time Miss Z. contacted Dr. Tart, she was experiencing OBEs nightly. At first he asked her to test herself at home. He told her to write the numbers one through ten on separate pieces of paper, shake them up in a box, and then choose one randomly—without looking at it—before she went to bed at night. She was to place the number on her nightstand. If she had an OBE during the night, she was to observe and memorize the number. She reported success seven nights in a row.

Tart then brought Miss Z. to the laboratory for monitored experiments similar to the ones he had conducted with Robert Monroe. As she lay in a bed, a random five-digit number on a piece of paper was placed out of sight behind her on a small shelf several feet above her head. She was instructed to read the number if she had an OBE. She was wired to an electroencephalograph (EEG) to chart her brain waves, and to other instruments that would measure her physiological condition during her reported OBEs. The wires were loose enough to allow her to turn over but would detach and interrupt the monitors if her physical body were to rise more than two feet, thus keeping her from seeing the number by ordinary means.

On the first night nothing happened. On the second night, at 3:15 A.M., the EEG revealed an unusual brain wave pattern. Miss Z. reported an OBE at that time, but she said she could not read the number. She had a similar experience on the third night.

The fourth night, however, was a different story. At 5:57 the EEG began to record disturbed brain waves that represented neither clear-cut sleeping nor waking. Shortly after 6:00, Miss Z. called in the technician, explained that she had undergone an OBE, and recited the digits 25132, the exact target sequence. The odds against this happening by chance were put at approximately 100,000 to 1. When

Tart reviewed the output from the other monitors, he found that during her reported out-of-body experience, Miss Z.'s pulse and brain-wave patterns did not slow down as they would in deep sleep and that REMs were absent, which indicated that she had not been dreaming. These findings were confirmed by Dr. William Dement, an expert on sleep states who later examined the data.

Like the Monroe experiments, the Miss Z. experiments did not offer irrefutable evidence that an OBE had taken place. For one thing, it was discovered that Miss Z. could have seen the number by shining a flashlight up at it and then reading its reflection on the glass face of a wall clock. Although there was no reason to suspect her of such trickery, the experiment remained flawed.

A more complicated problem with the design of Tart's experiments was that even if Miss Z. had correctly identified 1,000 targets, there would still be no proof that she had traveled out of her body to do so. Indeed, as some parapsychologists saw it, the same results could have been obtained through extrasensory perception, or ESP. For example, Miss Z. could have determined the correct number through clairvoyance, the alleged ability to receive images of people or things removed from natural sight.

This was a doubly intriguing possibility. For if clairvoyance could be claimed as a reality, then why not out-of-body travel? The existence of one would seem to lend credence to the other, in which case an obvious question arose: How would it ever be possible to distinguish an OBE from a clairvoyant experience? In the 1970s, Dr. Karlis Osis set out to answer that question at the American Society for Psychical Research in New York. Osis wanted to design experiments to see if OBE sight would be limited in the same way normal sight is, thus differentiating it from clairvoyance, which supposedly has no such limitations.

In 1972, Dr. Osis and his associate Janet Mitchell began a fourteen-month series of experiments with an artist named Ingo Swann. A large, blond, cigar-smoking man, Swann claimed to have had his first OBE at the age of two while under anesthesia for a tonsillectomy. Many more psy-

37

Artist Ingo Swann poses with his painting, *Aft Ship's View of Sagittarius*, inspired in part by his alleged astral expeditions to distant galaxies. Swann, who claims to be fully alert during his travels, seeks to convey in such art a sense of being in outer space.

actual black letter-opener case placed on top of it); the other picture was a three-colored bull's-eye, with a pie-shaped slice cut out of it. Swann reproduced both of these objects with remarkable accuracy. Even the pie-shaped slice was in the correct position. His only mistake was reversing the colors of the rings of the bull's-eye.

At other times, however, Swann had trouble identifying numbers, letters, or anything other than general shapes. He describes a failed but intriguing attempt in his autobiography, *To Kiss Earth Good-Bye.* "With the experiment well under way, I was once more trying valiantly to perceive what was in the box but the blackness I usually confronted did not subsequently resolve into the remote vision expected of it. Trying to figure out why everything 'looked' extraordinarily black, I 'floated' into the box itself (I was only supposed to peer through the aperture) and perceived that the small light used to illuminate the interior targets was not on. 'The goddamned light is out over the target,' I shouted, eager to catch the researchers in their inexpertise, as they were usually gleeful to catch me at a good failure. 'Impossible,' came the reply. Nonetheless, I stuck to my perceived response. When the trial was completed, a tall ladder was procured. When the target monitor clambered up it, he found that the light was not on."

Osis saw such unsuccessful attempts not necessarily as failures but rather as possible evidence that Swann was actually viewing the objects out-of-body and that out-of-body sight could indeed be limited by the same factors that interfere with physical vision. He believed that this differed from the vague and fragmented way in which alleged ESP messages are supposedly received and processed.

Osis decided to go one step further. He not only wanted to establish the relationship between OBE vision and physical sight but also hoped to produce some tangible proof of externalization—to show that a nonphysical self actually leaves the physical body during an OBE. Seeking to find such hard evidence, Osis began a new series of experiments with a specially developed optical image device.

chic voyages had followed, and he claimed to have reached a point where he could project himself out of his body while fully conscious.

In the Osis experiments, Swann would sit in an easy chair in a room illuminated by a soft overhead light, virtually immobilized by wires that hooked him up to a polygraph machine, which monitored his brain waves, respiration, and blood pressure. Puffing away on his cigar, he would, as he put it, "liberate his mind"; then he would be asked to describe or draw his impression of objects that were set out of sight in a box on a platform suspended from the ceiling.

During one session, two pictures were placed on the platform. One of them was an inverted red heart (with an

The apparatus measured three feet by two feet by two feet, with a viewing hole in one side. When looking through the hole, one saw a colored picture lying on one of four quadrants. But this was actually an optical illusion created by a series of mirrors, colored filters, and line drawings. The image in the device was in fact produced by a random number generator, activated by a push button in the adjacent room. Osis hypothesized that a subject having an OBE would see the optical illusion, whereas someone experiencing ESP or clairvoyance would mentally take the lid off the device and see the mirrors, filters, and line drawings instead of the optical illusion.

In 1978, together with psychic researcher Donna McCormick, Osis began an extensive series of tests with the optical image equipment. Osis's star subject was Alex Ta-

nous, an alleged psychic from Maine, who had at one time taught theology at St. John's University in Brooklyn. Tanous was a dark-haired, exotic-looking man with penetrating dark eyes and heavy brow. He had a reputation as a psychic and on several occasions had been called upon by police to use his powers in attempts to solve crimes or locate missing persons. Tanous believed that he projected a phantomlike double during his out-of-body experiences, and he claimed

Can animals detect the presence of astral beings? In a 1973 experiment to find out, researchers at the Psychical Research Foundation in Durham, North Carolina, monitored test subject Keith Harary (below) as he tried to project his astral self into a room where a kitten played. There the kitten's activities were closely monitored by research director Dr. Robert Morris (opposite page), and any changes in behavior were recorded. During Harary's alleged spiritual visits, the kitten reportedly was much calmer than usual.

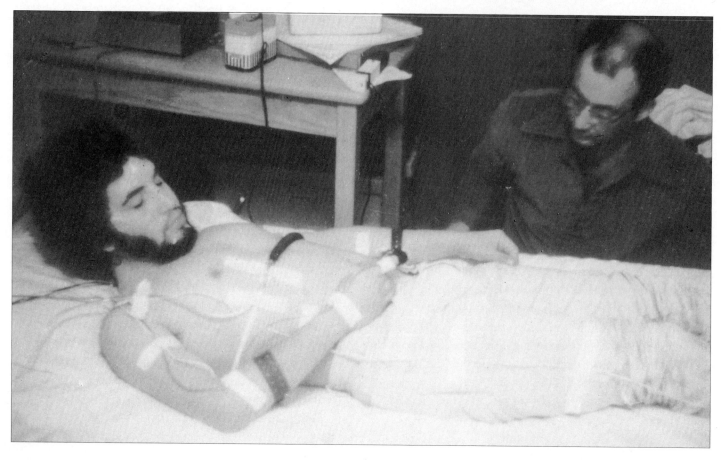

that this double could sometimes be seen by other people.

Upon arriving at ASPR's Manhattan headquarters, Tanous would typically come into Osis's office for a warming-up period. Over a cup of coffee, Osis and Tanous would discuss different aspects of the work under way to put Tanous into a positive frame of mind for the experiments. Tanous would then go to a sound-proof room. The targets he was to identify were located in the optical image device in a room at the opposite end of the building.

Tanous would attempt to project himself into the room to view the target, which could only be seen if he placed himself directly in front of the apparatus and looked in. To prove that the subject's double was, in fact, in the room, researchers also placed strain-gauge sensors that measured vibrations or motion in front of the optical device to track any sort of physical presence. A series of correct identifications by Tanous, coupled with positive sensor readings, would offer the strongest evidence to date of out-of-body journeying.

At first, the results were disappointing. But Tanous remained optimistic, concluding only that his out-of-body self was too small to see into the device. "When I first began working with the optical box," he said, "I couldn't see the target image because I wasn't tall enough—at least my other self wasn't tall enough. The window on the front of the optical box is at about eye level for a person of medium height. My projected self, my astral body, as I see it, has hardly any height at all. It's a small ball of light. I couldn't see into the window unless I strained, unless I 'stood on my tip toes'—even then, I couldn't see well."

Apparently Tanous's voyaging did not include floating weightlessly, although it did for many others. In any case, Osis obliged by building a platform for Tanous's nonphysical body to stand on. According to Osis, the results improved dramatically. In 197 trials conducted during twenty sessions, Tanous correctly identified the target 114 times. In addition, the vibration sensors reportedly showed a significantly higher level of activity when Tanous was correct.

At about the same time that Osis was conducting his experiments with Ingo Swann, an equally intriguing series of tests was being run at the Psychical Research Foundation, an independent research center in North Carolina. There the foundation's director of research, Dr. Robert Morris, was conducting some extensive experiments with a subject named Keith Harary, an intelligent, rational Duke University undergraduate who reported having had OBEs since childhood. Like Ingo Swann, Harary also claimed that he could voluntarily induce OBEs.

For the first series of experiments, Harary remained in one building while researchers hung large cardboard letters throughout another building twenty yards away. After the subject was wired to various monitoring devices, he was asked to lie down, relax, and allow his mind to travel. Because he was uneasy about being observed during his supposed OBEs, he usually projected from a closed booth. He would, however, signal researchers over an intercom when he was about to leave his body.

During some of these tests, Harary was amazingly accurate in sighting and describing the targets. At other times, his accuracy was poor. One day, however, there was an unusual development. During this particular test, only one volunteer was supposed to be in the room with the cardboard letter that Harary was trying to see. Unknown to Harary, a second volunteer was also in the room. While Harary failed to identify the target letter, he reported the presence of the second volunteer. More surprisingly, the second volunteer claimed to have seen Harary's apparition in the room.

Did this mean that Harary responded more readily to people than to cardboard letters? Fascinated by this possibility, foundation staff members devised a new experiment. Harary was again isolated in a closed booth in one building and was asked to project himself to a room in another building, where four staff members were gathered. Harary was to identify the people he saw there. He scored perfectly on the first attempt, not only identifying the participants but accurately reporting where each of the four was seated. Subsequent attempts yielded less spectacular results, but on occasion, some of the participants reported having sensed Harary's presence in the room. Even Morris claimed one such experience.

Perplexed about how to interpret these results, the research team attempted to record Harary's astrally projected presence in a room by gauging the reactions of animals. Recalling the popular belief that animals react oddly in haunted houses or when confronting ghosts, the researchers speculated that animals would also show altered behavior in the presence of a disembodied projection.

For the experiment, an animal would be placed in an animal activity board—a large, open box marked into twenty-four numbered ten-inch squares. Researchers would note the animal's normal activity rate by recording the frequency of its movement, the range of squares it passed over, and its noise level, and then determine whether these patterns changed when Harary made his alleged mental visits.

Harary was taken to a room at the Duke University Hospital, about a half mile from the testing center. One experimenter remained with him while he attempted to project himself into the room with the animal. Another experimenter monitored a kitten placed on the activity board. The kitten watcher was told that during the experiment, a phone in the room would ring four times. (Apparently, though, the researchers did not consider what effect the ringing phone might have on the animal.) Each time this occurred, he was to observe the kitten very carefully.

The experiment was run several times. Harary tried to project on only two of the occasions. During those two times, the observer saw the kitten suddenly stop running around and meowing and sit motionless.

To take the experiment one step further, Morris decided to study the reactions of a less-domesticated animal. Graham Watkins, an advisor on the project, had the perfect subject—a snake with a particularly vicious disposition. Morris reasoned that since the snake had such a negative reaction to humans in their physical bodies, it would likely have a similar reaction to a human in nonphysical state.

Harary was again taken to the Duke University Hospital, while two researchers observed the snake at the research center. The snake, in a terrarium, was placed in a small isolation booth and observed through a window. The experiment was run in a manner identical to the kitten experiment, with a phone call signaling the beginning of observation periods.

When the first period began, the snake was slithering about its terrarium in a normal fashion. With the second signal, however, the observer reported that the snake "slid up the side of the cage and literally seemed to attack the side of the terrarium. It bit at it wildly and then—just as mysteriously—calmed back down again. The response lasted about twenty or thirty seconds, and it was very startling." When researchers sought to duplicate the experiment a few days later, however, the snake burrowed under the shavings at the bottom of the terrarium and went to sleep even before the test began.

For all their painstaking ingenuity, none of the experiments yielded any proof that there is a second body that leaves the physical body during an OBE. But the results of these numerous tests and surveys have provided researchers with much food for thought, particularly considering the volume of reported OBEs. Some have concluded that an OBE may be a mental construct made up of recollections of the physical world, leavened with bits of information gleaned through telepathy or clairvoyance. But a number of psychologists have a more down-to-earth view, maintaining that apparent OBEs stem from a mental state called lucid dreaming—much like Calloway's "dreams of knowledge," where a person who is asleep and dreaming realizes that a dream is in progress. The dreamer thus believes that he or she is out of the body.

According to American anthropologist Dean Sheils, who has studied OBEs in sixty-seven different cultures around the world, sleep is regarded as the most important source of OBEs in about 80 percent of those cultures. Psychologist Stephen LaBerge, of the Stanford Sleep Research Center, goes on to hypothesize that since most OBEs occur

Glamorous Herald of a New Age

When actress and dancer Shirley MacLaine *(right)* announced to the world that she had lived an earlier life in Atlantis, had spoken to spirits through channelers, and believed that extraterrestrial beings had visited the earth, the growing New Age movement found a voice. A 1984 national survey showed that about two-thirds of all Americans claimed to have had some type of paranormal experience. Those numbers have increased in recent years, perhaps in part because of reports from people who were embarrassed to talk about their apparently psychic experiences until MacLaine came forward.

The actress, who says she has always had mystic leanings, was set on the path to inner enlightenment by helpful friends in the 1970s. But one of the most profound moments in her spiritual odyssey occurred during a 1975 trip to the Andes Mountains of Peru. There, sitting in a warm mineral bath by the soft glow of candlelight, MacLaine experienced her first out-of-body journey.

· "I breathed deeply," she would write later. "I stared at the flickering candle. My head felt light. I physically felt a kind of tunnel open in my mind. It grew like a cavern of clear space that was open and free of jumble. The flame of the candle slowly melted into the space in my mind. I felt myself *become* the flame. I had no arms, no legs, no body, no physical form. I felt myself flow into the space, fill it, and float off, rising out of my body until I began to soar. I was aware that my body remained in the water. I looked down and saw it. My spirit or mind or soul, or whatever it was, climbed higher into space. Right through the ceiling of the pool house and upward . . . until I could see the mountains and the landscape below me. I was aware, as I soared, of vibrational energy around me.

"I watched the silver cord attached to my body. It glistened in the air. It felt limitless in length, totally elastic, always attached to my body. My sight came from some kind of spiritual eye. I could see the curvature of the earth and darkness on the other side of the globe.

"I directed myself downward, back to my body. The energy vibrations subsided, and with a soft fusion of contact that felt like a puff, I melded back into my body."

MacLaine says her out-of-body experience made her feel like an "individualized piece of Universal Energy." And she believes she has been selected by entities in the spirit world to carry the message of enlightenment to others. After publishing accounts of her spiritual awakening in two bestselling books, she starred in a television drama based on her story. And for others wishing to "achieve alignment with the energies of the New Age," MacLaine began conducting a series of seminars around the country. The workshops, which include group meditations, visualization techniques, and questions and answers relating to past lives, "made it all right for people who've been thinking about these things in private to do them with less fear and ridicule," she says.

MacLaine and other leaders of the New Age movement—a loosely defined philosophy that espouses a variety of mystical beliefs, including the idea that the soul survives bodily death—have gained a wide following. Although the movement is generally viewed as harmless, it is not without its critics. For instance, possibly the fastest-growing technique for New Age awareness involves channeling, a method by which self-proclaimed psychics reportedly act as conduits for spirits from another world or time. Some critics categorize these supposed mediums as con artists taking advantage of typically well-educated and affluent —but somewhat credulous—people trying to find some meaning in their lives.

Even some devotees will admit that the psychic field can be riddled with frauds, but interest continues unabated. For Shirley MacLaine, embracing the visions of the New Age has meant a new way of looking at life and at herself. "I know I have lived past lives," she says. "I know there is life before birth. I can't prove that, but then I couldn't have proved that I had microbes on my arm until the microscope was invented."

during sleep, they are actually variant interpretations of lucid dreams. And he supports his conclusion with his own experience: "In about one percent of the lucid dreams in my record, I felt I was in some sense out of my body. In every case, when examining the experience after awakening, I noted some deficiency in either my memory or my critical thinking during the experience. In one such situation, I tried to memorize the serial number of a dollar bill to verify later whether I really had been out of my body or not. When I awoke, I couldn't recall the number, but it hardly mattered. I remembered that I hadn't lived in the house I thought I was asleep in for several years."

Others, however, disagree with the theory that an OBE can be explained as a form of lucid dream. Psychic researcher Susan Blackmore, for one, contends that the experiments with Robert Monroe, Keith Harary, and Ingo Swann all have shown that while the subjects are usually very relaxed, physiological indicators such as heart rate, eye movement, and EEG readings prove that they are not fully asleep. Blackmore therefore concludes that OBEs cannot be considered a kind of dreaming. She contends, instead, that they are created by an "altered state of consciousness, related to other altered states such as dreams and drug states, but having special characteristics."

Another researcher, a psychiatrist by the name of Glen Gabbard, speculates that out-of-body experiences may, in fact, be what he calls hypnagogic images—images that occur during the time one hovers between wakefulness and sleep. He concludes that the hypnagogic image is experienced as extremely real, and this causes it to be confused with an actual experience outside the body.

Whatever they are, supposed OBEs often exert a profound impact on those who have experienced them. Many people emerge with entirely new values and beliefs, often convinced of the reality of life after death and a world beyond the senses. One of the most notable of these is Shirley MacLaine, the Academy Award-winning actress. A tireless traveler and writer, MacLaine had explored and recorded many supposedly paranormal phenomena before she experienced her own OBE while on a spiritual pilgrimage in the Andes. During the episode, she said, she floated so high out of her physical body that she found herself in space gazing down at the curve of the earth. On another occasion she reported that she felt the presence of her friend Peter Sellers in her living room in Malibu, California, at the moment the actor died of a heart attack in England.

MacLaine's autobiographical accounts of her spiritual quest, *Out on a Limb* and *Dancing in the Light,* have been read by millions, and she has conducted numerous workshops for people interested in OBEs and spiritual awareness. She appeals to a whole network of believers gathered around the world in groups dedicated to exploring realms beyond the normal senses. Known collectively as part of the New Age movement, these people see it as their mission to promote widespread acceptance of an independent soul as a means of improving humankind's life on earth.

Their efforts recall the hopes expressed in the 1920s by psychic researcher Archibald Holms: "A widespread conviction of continued existence after death and of the temporary character of earth life would do much to ameliorate conditions in the latter. The outlook on life would be different, things now regarded as of paramount importance would cease to be so regarded; unscrupulous ambition, the passion for wealth and power over one's fellow-men, and the desire of social distinction, would all be robbed of their glamour, to the great good of the individual and the masses."

Recent scientific developments, particularly in theoretical physics, may open the way to these possibilities as well. Concepts such as black holes and antimatter, after all, are as strange in their own way as the notion of astral travel. Meanwhile, New Agers and others can turn to reports of still more forms of out-of-body experience to bolster their beliefs in the existence of a soul that is independent of the physical body. Among the most intriguing reports of such phenomena are those of people who have allegedly broken free of their bodies and journeyed to the very gates of death itself, only to return once more to the land of the living.

Phases of an OBE

"I found myself in a state of ecstasy, a state of great joy, and I was amazed by the power that was propelling me, as if it could move anything in the universe."

Thus did one seasoned astral traveler describe the onset of a supposed out-of-body episode—as a form of *ecstasy*, a word traceable to Greek roots that literally means to stand outside of one's self. And indeed, out-of-body experiences lend figurative and literal dimension to the phrase "beside oneself with joy." Most studies show that the majority of people claiming to have had the experience describe it as pleasant, fascinating, even joyful. After an initial episode, most of them want to try it again.

However, an aspiring voyager should not overlook occasional reports describing OBEs as nightmarish. One young woman, for example, told of feeling pulled from her body by a force that was so strong she feared her heart would be ripped from her chest. Sensations of pain, pressure, and terror persisted throughout her experience, which left lasting psychological damage. At the very least, the first few out-of-body voyages are often said to be frightening. A common dread is that the traveler may become permanently detached from the physical body and die, though no such misadventure has been reported. There are also accounts of unpleasant physical side effects, including a burning sensation and a racing heart when the astral self reenters the body.

Some of the highlights of a more typically idyllic out-of-body experience are illustrated on the following pages.

The astral voyager feels her body becoming rigid, immobile. She has the frustrating sensation of being unable to command her own limbs. But this feeling of helplessness diminishes once the spirit body has completely separated from the physical one. The voyager sees a silver cord connecting the physical self with its etheric counterpart, a cord whose original thickness attenuates as distance increases between the two selves.

Though the astral body seems weightless, insubstantial, its powers of perception are unimpaired, perhaps even preternaturally sharp. The astral self sees unusually bright, vivid colors. She senses that her disembodied form, though nonphysical, has a strange vitality missing from what she thinks of as her real body. Indeed, it is the astral self that begins to seem real, the physical body only a shell.

The astral traveler apprehends her own insubstantiality only when she attempts an ordinary physical function—opening a door—and finds herself able to penetrate solid objects. There is a sense of shock, followed by delight, as she begins to realize that limitations of the physical world need no longer apply. Her will is her compass and her vehicle. To wish herself elsewhere is to journey there.

The length of out-of-body journeys is said to vary a great deal. Some voyagers, frightened by the extraordinary circumstance of the OBE, may stray only a few feet and for only a few moments from the physical body before hastening to reenter it. The more venturesome traveler, on the other hand, finds pleasure in testing and extending the experience's limits, reveling in its freedom, soaring far and wide.

Pleasurable as the experience is, the voyager eventually feels anxious about straying too far from the physical body, of losing touch with it and thus being set adrift in an alien realm. There is a sense that while the spirit—the disembodied self—will survive in some astral form, the abandoned earthbound body will die. The fear seems to prompt a return, instantly pulling the spirit self back to its physical host. The two merge, and the voyager rejoins mundane reality.

CHAPTER 2

At the Portal of Death

arly in December 1943, as American troops fought the Japanese in the Solomon Islands, and as the Allies prepared to invade Normandy, a twenty-year-old army private named George Ritchie celebrated his good luck. He could hardly believe that, after finishing basic training in Abilene, Texas, he was to go to the Medical College of Virginia, where he would become a doctor at government expense.

Seven days before he was to leave for medical school, Private Ritchie developed a bad chest cold. It turned into influenza, and he was hospitalized. Over the next few days he seemed to recover. But the night before he was scheduled to leave for Richmond, his temperature soared to a life-threatening 106.5 degrees Fahrenheit. His surroundings became a dizzy blur. He heard the click and whir of the X-ray machine—and then silence.

The young soldier woke up on a strange bed in a small, dimly lit, unfamiliar room. His head was clear. In a panic that he might miss the train to Richmond, Private Ritchie jumped out of bed. "My uniform wasn't on the chair," he remembered later. "I looked beneath it. Behind it. No duffel bag either . . . . Under the bed maybe? I turned around, then froze."

Ritchie was shocked to see that a young man was lying in the bed that he had just vacated. "The thing was impossible," he recalled. "I myself had just gotten out of that bed. For a moment I wrestled with the mystery of it. It was too strange to think about—and anyway, I didn't have time."

Private Ritchie shivered and ran from the room. The only thing he could think about was getting to Richmond. Out in the hall a sergeant walked toward him carrying an instrument tray. "Excuse me, Sergeant," Ritchie said. "You haven't seen the ward boy for this unit, have you?" The sergeant did not answer or even slow down. At the last minute Ritchie yelled, "Look out!" but the man walked right past him. The next minute he was behind him, walking away without even looking back at Ritchie.

Before he had time to wonder if he was delirious or dreaming, Ritchie found himself outside the hospital. It was dark and he was moving fast, as though flying through the air. He still wore only his army hospital pajamas but had no sensation of cold. After willing himself to slow down, Ritchie landed on a street corner in a town by a large river. People walked by without seeing him. He leaned up against a thick guy wire bracing a telephone pole, but his body passed right through it. "In some unimaginable way," George Ritchie wrote later, "I had lost my firmness of flesh, the body that other people saw."

Oddly, given the bizarre circumstances, the young man's most pressing concern was that he was not going to be able to study medicine in his present disembodied form. He knew he had to get back to his physical body as fast as he could. The return to the hospital was quick, even faster than his voyage away from it had been. Running from ward to ward and room to room, Ritchie searched the faces of sleeping soldiers. It was not easy to distinguish them in the dim light, so he decided to look for his identifying onyx and gold fraternity ring on their hands instead.

After what seemed an eternity, Private Rit-

chie found a left hand with the correct ring on the third finger, but the body was covered with a sheet. For the first time he thought, "This is what we human beings call 'death,' this splitting up of one's self." At the same time, he wondered how he could be dead and still be awake, thinking and experiencing.

Suddenly, the room was filled with an intense illumination, and Ritchie saw that a man made of light had appeared. From inside himself he heard the words, "You are in the presence of the Son of God." Simultaneously, his whole life, "every event and thought and conversation, as palpable as a series of pictures," he said later, passed before him in review.

Then Private Ritchie woke up in his own body, to the astonishment of the physician who had just signed his death certificate. An orderly who had been preparing the body for the morgue noticed fee-

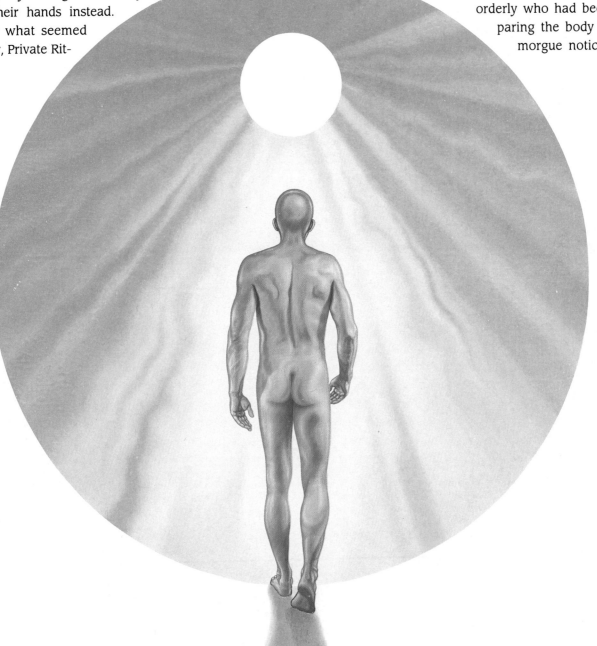

ble signs of life in the corpse and called the doctor, who hastily injected adrenalin directly into the heart. Although Ritchie had not taken a breath for nine full minutes, he showed no symptoms of brain damage. The commanding officer at the hospital called the Ritchie case "the most amazing circumstance" of his career and signed an affidavit that George Ritchie had indeed made a miraculous return from virtual death on the night of December 20, 1943.

Private George Ritchie went on to become Dr. George

Such anecdotal evidence, available from sources throughout the world and throughout history, has attracted scientific notice since Victorian times. However, it was not until the twentieth century, when advances in medical technology made it possible to revive people who were apparently dead, that this research received much in the way of popular notice. During recent decades the medical profession has been unable to ignore the accounts of those who, when threatened with death, apparently had experiences in

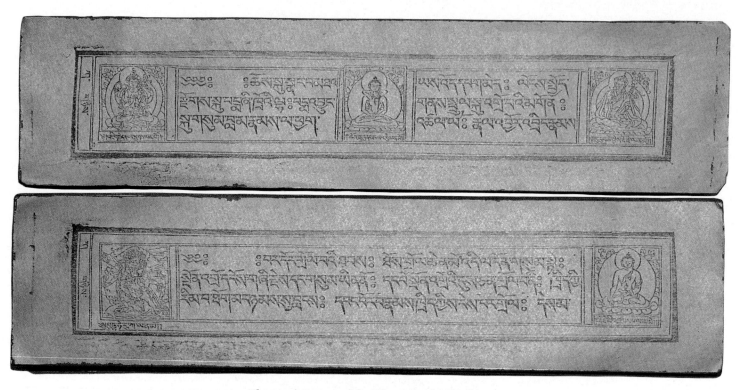

The opening pages of the Tibetan Bardo Thodol, or
Book of the Dead, pay homage to Buddha in his various manifestations—represented
in the drawings—and introduce the process of preparing
for death and the after-death experience.

Ritchie, a psychiatrist who had ample opportunity to study dreams and hallucinations. Such work convinced him that his own extraordinary experience was no delusion—that he had, in fact, seen over the threshold of death. Nor, it appears, was his mystic journey unique. No less a realist than the author Ernest Hemingway, after he was wounded in Italy during World War I, felt his soul leave his body; he later used some of his memories of it in the novel *A Farewell to Arms (pages 10-11)*. Famed aviator Edward V. ("Eddie") Rickenbacker, rescued after three weeks on a raft in the Pacific Ocean in 1942, recounted in his autobiography how he had faced death: "Then I began to die, I felt the presence of death, and I knew that I was going . . . . All was serene and calm. How wonderful it would be simply to float out of this world. It is easy to die."

which they felt as if their spirits were somehow moving toward an afterlife. In the 1970s and 1980s, these near-death experiences, or NDEs, as they came to be called, were brought to public attention in books and lectures by such investigators as Raymond A. Moody, Jr., Kenneth Ring, and Elisabeth Kübler-Ross.

Increasingly rigorous analysis of these stories has shown many of them to be remarkably consistent. Furthermore, those who recount them are almost always sincere people whose experiences do not appear to be delusions or dreams. Still, researchers have been unable to demonstrate the objective reality of near-death experiences, and the jury is still out on their significance. Most people who are facing death do not report such occurrences. Are those who do merely suffering from stress-induced hallucinations? Or are their real-seeming experiences real in fact, thereby demonstrating the separate existence of the consciousness and the presence of a world beyond death?

The idea of voyaging to an afterlife is nothing new. Cro-Magnon people buried their dead with weapons and food, suggesting that they were preparing the deceased for another existence. By the time of Plato, such a notion had evolved into detailed stories. In Book X of *The Republic,* written nearly 400 years before the birth of Christ, the philosopher tells an allegorical story of a soldier named Er, who fell in battle. Ten days later, when the corpses were being collected, most of them were rotting, but Er's body was not. Plato writes: "When they had carried him home . . . on the twelfth day, being laid on the [funeral] pyre, he came to life again." And then, according to Plato, Er began to tell his startled listeners of the things he had witnessed in a world beyond life.

First, Er said, his soul went out of his body, and he joined with a group of other souls. They went to a place where there were passageways leading into the realms of the afterlife. Here the other spirits were held and judged by divine beings who could perceive everything that the soul had done while in its earthly body. Er, the soldier, was not judged. Instead he was informed that it was not yet his time and that he must return to tell those in the physical realm what the world beyond was like. After being shown many other strange and wonderful sights, Er was sent back. He could not explain how he traveled; he simply woke up and found himself on the funeral pyre about to be cremated.

Plato's tale, while it is clearly mythological, illustrates the sequence of near-death events that was to become so familiar in later centuries. A similar multistage journey appears in the eighth-century Tibetan Book of the Dead, representing the collective wisdom of generations of Tibetan holy men. The sages who contributed to the book believed that dying was an art, something that one could learn to do well. Read to the dying in the last minutes of life, or even to the dead at the funeral, the Tibetan Book of the Dead prepared the person for the experience to come. Its words could also help the still-living to think positive thoughts and to refrain from holding the dying one back with their love and concern.

The similarity that exists between the early stages of death as they were described by the Tibetan sages and the typical twentieth-century near-death experience is remarkable. According to the Tibetans, those who are approaching death first find themselves suspended in a void. Still conscious, they may hear galelike roaring and whistling noises. A misty, gray light sometimes surrounds them.

The dying then become aware that they have left their physical body. Surprised, they do not believe it at first, because they feel unchanged. And when they see and hear grieving relatives and friends preparing for a funeral, the now-deceased try to talk to their loved ones but get no response. Finally, realizing their perplexing situation, they notice that they do still have a body of sorts, a shining, immaterial form. In this condition, they discover they can pass through solid rock without hindrance. And travel is a simple matter of wishing to be somewhere.

As the spirits move toward a realm of light, they slough off emotional attachments to their earthly existence. In the process, they may face spiritual beings who judge them, and who present them with a kind of mirror reflecting their life and actions. Filled at last with peace and contentment, the deceased prepare either to abandon the world altogether or to reenter the round of birth and death with a higher awareness of the illusory nature of life.

Like the Tibetans, Western philosophers and visionaries often describe a separation of body and soul at death. Christian mystics have described how, when near death from illness or accident, their spirits were guided by angels through a tour of hell and heaven and their actions were weighed. Their journeys often ended in a realm of light.

These visionaries interpreted their near-death experiences as religious events. Beginning in the late nineteenth century, however, a few researchers began to collect together such stories and to develop a secular description of the phenomenon.

One such was Albert Heim, a Swiss professor of geology and an avid mountain climber whose studies were inspired by his own brush with death. While climbing the Säntis Mountain in the Swiss Alps in 1871, Heim slipped and fell from the edge of a cliff. Though he survived the accident, he was certain at the time that he was going to die. Describing the experience later, he wrote:

What followed was a series of singularly clear flashes of thought between a rapid, profuse succession of images that were sharp and distinct . . . . I can perhaps compare it best to images from film sprung loose in a projector or with the rapid sequence of dream images. As though I looked out of the window of a high house, I saw myself as a seven-year-old boy going to school. Then I saw myself in the classroom with my beloved teacher Weisz, in fourth grade. I acted out my life, as though I were an actor on stage, upon which I looked down as though from practically the highest gallery in the theater. I was both hero and onlooker . . . . I had the feeling of submission to necessity. Then I saw arching over me—my eyes were directed upwards—a beautiful blue heaven with small violet and rosy-red clouds. Then sounded solemn music, as though from an organ, in powerful chords . . . . I felt myself go softly backwards into this magnificent heaven—without anxiety, without grief. It was a great, glorious moment!"

His interest piqued, Heim went on to seek out the stories of others who had reported similar experiences, and in 1892 he published an article that analyzed the accounts of more than thirty survivors of near-fatal falls in the Alps. His study was one of the first to identify some common elements of near-death experiences, among them the amazing expansion of time, the review of one's life, and the extraordinary sensations of peace and even joy experienced in what seemed to be one's last moments.

At the same time that Heim was examining the emotions of climbers facing death, scientists inspired by the growing spiritualism movement took another approach to the study of mortality. These researchers, many of them with impeccable scientific credentials, began to investigate the existence of ghosts and apparitions. In the process, some of them became interested in deathbed visions.

One such investigator was Sir William Barrett, a physicist at the Royal College of Science in Dublin. He began collecting deathbed visions in the 1920s after his wife, an obstetrician, reported an unusual case to him.

On the night of January 12, 1924, Lady Barrett delivered the baby of a woman named Doris. (The Barretts withheld her last name when reporting the story.) After the difficult birth, as the woman lay dying, she looked toward one part of the room with a radiant smile. "Oh, lovely, lovely," she said. When asked what was lovely, Doris replied, "What I *see.*" She spoke in a low, intense voice. "Lovely brightness—wonderful beings."

Then, Lady Barrett reported, Doris seemed to focus on one spot in the room and cried out, "Why, it's Father! Oh, he's so glad I'm coming; he is so glad. It would be perfect if only W. [her husband, his name also concealed by the Barretts] would come too."

Doris's baby was brought for her to see. She looked at it with concern, and then said, "Do you think I ought to stay for baby's sake?" Turning toward her vision, she cried, "I can't—I can't stay; if you could see what I do, you would know I can't stay." Speaking presumably to her father, she said, "I am coming" and then, puzzled, commented to the bystanders, "He has Vida with him." Looking back to her vision, she said: "You do want me, Dad; I am coming."

The woman died shortly afterward. Aside from the sheer intensity of Doris's feelings and speech, what made the greatest impression on Sir William and Lady Barrett was the fact that Vida, Doris's sister, had died three weeks earlier—but Doris had not been told because of her precarious health. Doris, it seems, had had a vision of someone she could not have expected to see.

This episode, and a number of others like it, appeared in the book *Death-Bed Visions,* written by Sir William Barrett

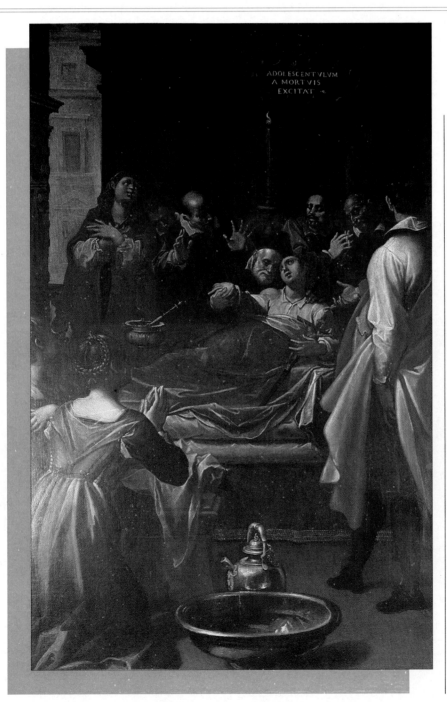

ADOLESCENTVLVM
A MORTVIS
EXCITAT

A Glimpse of the Beyond

As day was breaking on March 16, 1589, the mood inside the Rome palace of Italy's Prince Fabrizio Massimo was somber. The prince's son, fourteen-year-old Paolo, was deathly ill with a fever that had resisted all treatment. That morning, family members sent for a priest.

Father Filippo Neri, who presided at a nearby church, was considered an extraordinary holy man. He was said to have levitated during Mass, carried out exorcisms, and brought a number of people back from death. The priest was Paolo's confessor and had spent long hours in prayer with him during the boy's illness. Unfortunately, Paolo Massimo died thirty minutes before the priest could reach his bedside.

Anguished by the tragic loss of the prince's son, Father Filippo knelt in prayer for the young soul and blessed the still body with holy water. Then he leaned over and blew into Paolo's face and, placing his hand on the boy's forehead, twice called Paolo's name in a loud voice. As if by miracle, the young man opened his eyes, an event commemorated (left) by the sixteenth-century painter Il Pomarancio.

Paolo told those assembled in his room that he had been in heaven. He claimed he had seen his mother, who had died eight years earlier, and his recently deceased sister. It was a beautiful place, Paolo said, and he wanted to return. "Well then," intoned the priest, "go in peace and be blessed." Paolo then closed his eyes and quietly died.

in 1926. Familiar with the medical belief that dying patients see only hallucinations, Barrett pointed out that deathbed visions often occur when the patient's mind is clear and rational. Furthermore, the dying are often astonished by what they see; for example, Barrett wrote, dying children were surprised to see angels without wings. If their visions were hallucinations, he noted, they would be more likely to conform to popular stereotypes.

At the time Barrett collected his stories, investigators were more interested in communication with the dead than they were in the experiences of the dying. Thirty years later, however, Barrett's anecdotal book would inspire the parapsychologist Karlis Osis to undertake the first scientific studies of deathbed visions. And Doris's report of welcoming relatives at the threshold of death would in time become recognized as a feature of many a near-death experience.

Osis had long been interested in apparitions and extrasensory communication. While working with the Parapsychology Foundation in New York City in the late 1950s, he decided to follow up on some of Barrett's findings by talking to doctors and nurses who had regular oppportunities to observe patients in the process of dying.

His survey, conducted in 1959 and 1960, used modern statistical methods to show that deathbed visions had little in common with hallucinations: The visions were not influenced by drugs or fevers, Osis concluded, and the visual nature of the subject matter of such experiences differed from the auditory hallucinations that are typical of the mentally ill. Also, deathbed visions were two or three times more likely to be populated with dead people than were the apparitions reported by people who were not dying. The patients' age, social status, education, and religion seemed to have little effect on what they saw.

By the 1970s Osis had moved to the American Society for Psychical Research, where he was joined by another scientist with an interest in the paranormal, Icelandic psychologist Erlendur Haraldsson. Using Osis's first survey as a model, the two men conducted a new study of deathbed experiences, broadening their scope to include doctors and nurses in both the United States and India—two nations with very different cultural expectations and religious beliefs. Of 1,708 people questioned, about half reported deathbed observations and were interviewed in detail.

In both American and Indian cases, those who saw apparitions characteristically described them as messengers from beyond who had appeared to guide the patient over to the other world. The encounter with these beings was usually so pleasant that the value of earthly life was easily forgotten. In fact, in some cases patients seemed to die in accordance with the call of the apparition, even when doctors expected them to recover. A substantial minority, however—29 percent—reported negative experiences such as resisting the spirit or feeling threatened by it.

Interestingly, there were no major differences between American and Indian patients. But some minor ones did stand out. For example, a third of the dying Indians decided, apparently for religious reasons, not to heed the call of the apparition, whereas nearly all of the Americans were eager to go with it—that is, to die. The people who appeared to the Indians were mostly religious figures, while Americans usually reported dead relatives or friends.

The two parapsychologists decided that the visionary experience in America and India was essentially the same, although it was interpreted according to societal expectations. "We interpret these modest cultural differ-

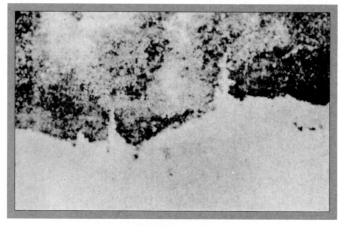

Nine hours after his son's death in the year 1907, the French psychical researcher Hippolyte Baraduc photographed the boy as he lay in his coffin. Baraduc, who claimed to have conversed with his son's apparition, explained the formless, misty mass in the photograph as the departed soul of his son.

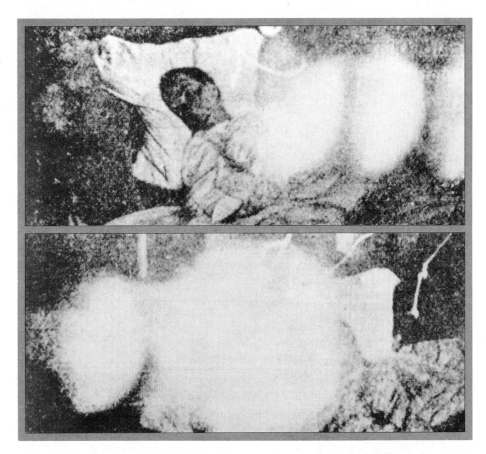

As Hippolyte Baraduc's wife died—six months after the death of the couple's son—she breathed three gentle sighs; Baraduc's photograph of that final moment shows three luminous globes hovering over her body (top). In a later image (above), the globes, which Baraduc believed to be his wife's soul, appear to be combined as one.

ences according to our model: they seem to support the hypothesis that deathbed visions are, in part, based on extrasensory perception of some form of external reality rather than having entirely subjective origins." The Osis-Haraldsson study, published in 1977, did not conclude that deathbed experiences prove life after death. It did say, however, that the existing data were more consistent with transition than extinction.

Other researchers disagreed with such findings. One of them, Russell Noyes, Jr., a professor of psychiatry at the University of Iowa, made his own study of the experiences of the dying and interpreted his data quite differently. To Noyes, mystical occurrences at the hour of death are a reflection of purely internal reality.

Like Professor Heim before him, Noyes spoke to people whose close brush with death was usually the result of an accident—although not all were injured. Many of the 104 subjects reported the peaceful sensations and life review noted by Heim. For instance, a twenty-one-year-old college student described her feelings as her car spun out of control toward a bridge abutment:

"I entered a calm dreamlike state accompanied by a feeling of being at peace with everything. Then I saw an endless stream of past experiences—there must have been hundreds—go through my mind. All sound seemed to blur into an indescribable monotone . . . . It seemed to take forever for everything to happen. Space too was unreal. It was all very much like sitting in a movie theater and watching it happen on the screen."

Noyes's work, conducted in the 1970s, marked a shift toward the medical and away from the parapsychological approach in near-death studies. The psychiatrist's conclusions reflect the Freudian view that one's unconscious is convinced of immortality and that death is unimaginable. Both the life review and the out-of-body sensation, Noyes believes, are devices of the mind to escape from the reality of death, ways of pretending that one is only a spectator.

According to Noyes, such an escape occurs when the neural mechanism of the brain produces feelings of depersonalization and hyperalertness, the first serving to eliminate emotion and the second to intensify attention. Depersonalization can produce a feeling of being detached from one's body and may cause one to hear strange sounds and experience an altered sense of time. Hyperalertness brings with it accelerated thoughts, sharper vision and hearing, and time distortion. In Noyes's view, these responses reflect a natural adaptive reaction that aids survival by dampening frantic emotion, allowing a person to cope calmly in a crisis. However, critics who favor a life-after-death thesis have responded that the psychiatrist's theories are as speculative as all others, and note that his proposals also fail to account for cases in which the dying see relatives whom they did not know to be dead.

At about the same time that Noyes was interviewing his 104 close calls, another student of the death experience, Dr. Elisabeth Kübler-Ross, made the issue famous. Trained as a psychiatrist, Kübler-Ross lifted the virtual public taboo on discussions of death and dying with her best-selling books in the late 1960s and afterward; her name would ever after be linked with the subject in the public mind. And while her books dealt primarily with the stages of acceptance of death, Kübler-Ross's work led her to believe in an afterlife. "Before I started working with dying patients," said Kübler-Ross in 1974, "I did not believe in life after death. I now believe in it beyond a shadow of a doubt."

Born in Zurich in 1926, the first of triplets, young Elisabeth Kübler had a closer acquaintance than most young women with death and suffering. Stubborn and independent, as a teenager she defied her father's wishes in order to nurse refugees from countries that had been devastated by World War II; later, she volunteered to treat survivors of the Holocaust in Poland. The horrors she saw there haunted her dreams for years.

After taking her medical degree at the University of Zurich (again, against her father's wishes), Kübler married an American doctor, Emanuel Ross, in 1958 and moved to the United States to specialize in psychiatry. Her work with terminally ill patients in Chicago persuaded her that the whole subject of death should be confronted and discussed much more openly. Having identified what she believed were the five emotional stages of dying—denial, anger, bargaining, depression, and acceptance—Kübler-Ross published her first book, *On Death and Dying,* in 1969 to widespread acclaim.

Yet even as she was gathering praise and writing sequels to her successful volume, Kübler-Ross's life was taking a turn away from the main-

In numerous near-death experience studies in the United States and India, parapsychologist Karlis Osis found that for many people death is attended by experiences of exaltation. The results of his cross-cultural surveys revealed a number of similarities, strongly suggesting to him that NDEs are not hallucinations.

stream of the medical profession. Some of the patients she had worked with reported mystical experiences as they neared death—and soon Kübler-Ross had some of her own. Not the least of them, by Kübler-Ross's account, came in the late 1960s, after she heard an unusual story from a dying woman by the name of Mrs. Schwartz.

Mrs. Schwartz told Kübler-Ross how, when she lay unconscious from internal bleeding, she regained awareness and found herself floating above her body. She could see everything in the room—the doctors, the nurses, their attempts to resuscitate her—but she could not speak to them. Mrs. Schwartz said she reentered her body as it was being wheeled to the morgue, and she startled the attendants by pulling the sheet away from her head.

Shortly after recounting this incident to Kübler-Ross, Mrs. Schwartz died. Around this time, the psychiatrist said, the stress of working with the dying was telling on her, and she decided to give up her specialty. As she stood in a hospital corridor, having just made her decision, she turned to see none other than Mrs. Schwartz beside her. The dead woman looked solid and real.

Kübler-Ross says she led her visitor to her office and asked her to write and sign a note as evidence of her visit. The smiling woman did so, then walked out of the room. Later, according to Kübler-Ross, the handwriting was compared with other samples of the dead woman's hand and identified as hers.

As time went by, the doctor became convinced of a higher reality of the spirit. After an all-night workshop for the dying in the mid-1970s, Kübler-Ross retired to her room in exhaustion. As soon as she lay down, however, she claims that her inner self left her body and looked down on a remarkable sight. A team of spirits was overhauling her body, removing worn-out parts and replacing them with fresh material. When she woke up, back in her body, she says, she felt better than she had in years.

After studying such experiences, says Kübler-Ross, she learned to induce her own out-of-body experiences whenever she wanted. Combining her studies of death and dying with such personal episodes, the psychiatrist started to speak out publicly on the separate existence of the spirit and the reality of the afterlife. "When people die," she said, "they very simply shed their body, much as a butterfly comes out of its cocoon."

Such pronouncements gained for Kübler-Ross the suspicion of formerly admiring medical colleagues. Her reputation plummeted further in the late 1970s, when she joined with a former aircraft worker named Jay Barham to found a forty-two-acre retreat in California devoted to workshops on death and dying. Barham, said the doctor, was a natural healer and medium. Spirits supposedly cloned themselves from the cells of his body.

Disgruntled participants in retreat workshops reported a different story, however. According to some women, Barham's real mission was to lure them into a dark room where, disguised as a so-called entity, he would pursuade them to have sex with him. Nevertheless, Kübler-Ross remained serenely confident of the ultimate truth of her visions and claimed to ignore her critics. By the mid-1980s, she had moved into the treatment of AIDS patients—still convinced that an afterlife awaits the dying.

Despite her forays into questionable spiritualism, no one would deny that Elisabeth Kübler-Ross did much to advance popular understanding of death and dying. And her work also set the stage for what may have been the most influential book on the near-death experience: Raymond Moody's *Life after Life*, published in 1975. Moody has been criticized for his unscientific, anecdotal approach to the subject, but it was he who first categorized the common features of many near-death experiences (a phrase he coined) and who clarified the concept for the public. His book, as well as Kübler-Ross's studies, has given the average person the clearest picture yet of what it is like to die.

Raymond Moody was first exposed to the subject in the middle of the 1960s, when he was a philosophy student at the University of Virginia and heard Dr. George Ritchie, a professor of psychiatry at the school, describe his own near-death experience as a soldier in Texas during World War II. Ritchie said that he had been allowed to return to this life so that he could learn more about humanity and then serve God. After receiving his doctorate in philosophy, Moody went on to teach in North Carolina, and there he heard his second account of a near-death experience from a student whose story was remarkably similar to Ritchie's. By the time he entered medical school in 1972, Moody had begun to gather together an informal collection of such reports. He found these near-death stories to be so widespread, and yet so little studied, that he decided to conduct his own survey and interviews as he was beginning his medical career.

Moody collected about 150 tales. Some of them came from people who were resuscitated after having been declared dead. Others were the accounts of people who, through accident or severe illness, had come very close to death. After studying these firsthand stories, Moody identified fifteen elements that recurred among the NDEs. Not all of them were present in any one case, nor did they necessarily occur in the same sequence. However, a theoretically ideal or complete near-death experience would, in Moody's words, run something like this:

"A man is dying and, as he reaches the point of greatest physical distress, he hears himself pronounced dead by his doctor. He begins to hear an uncomfortable noise, a loud ringing or buzzing, and at the same time feels himself moving very rapidly through a long dark tunnel. After this, he suddenly finds himself outside of his own physical body, but still in the immediate physical environment, and he sees his own body from a distance, as though he is a spectator. He watches the resuscitation attempt from this unusual vantage point and is in a state of emotional upheaval.

"After a while, he collects himself and becomes more accustomed to his odd condition. He notices that he still has a 'body,' but one of a very different nature and with very different powers from the physical body he has left behind.

Psychiatrist Elisabeth Kübler-Ross, shown here with a terminally ill patient, documented hundreds of near-death experiences. Later, she began speaking publicly—and with conviction—about life after death.

Soon other things begin to happen. Others come to meet and to help him. He glimpses the spirits of relatives and friends who have already died, and a loving, warm spirit of a kind he has never encountered before—a being of light—appears before him. This being asks him a question, nonverbally, to make him evaluate his life and helps him along by showing him a panoramic, instantaneous playback of the major events of his life. At some point he finds himself approaching some sort of barrier or border, apparently representing the limit between earthly life and the next life. Yet, he finds that he must go back to the earth, that the time for his death has not yet come. At this point he resists, for by now he is taken up with his experiences in the afterlife and does not want to return. He is overwhelmed by intense feelings of joy, love, and peace. Despite his attitude, though, he somehow reunites with his physical body and lives.

"Later he tries to tell others, but he has trouble doing so. In the first place, he can find no human words adequate to describe these unearthly episodes. He also finds that others scoff, so he stops telling other people. Still, the experience affects his life profoundly, especially his views about death and its relationship to life."

Moody also described each of the characteristic elements of the NDEs he heard. The main features are:

Ineffability. Moody found that those who reported NDEs uniformly believe them to be inexpressible in ordinary language. As one woman put it, "Our world—the one we're living in now—*is* three-dimensional, but the next one definitely isn't. And that's why it's so hard to tell you this. I have to describe it to you in words that are three-dimensional. That's as close as I can get to it, but it's not really adequate. I can't really give you a complete picture."

Hearing the news of one's own death. Many of Moody's respondents tell of hearing their doctors or others pronounce them dead. Said one survivor: "First, they tested this drug they were going to use on my arm, since I had a lot of drug allergies. But there was no reaction, so they went ahead. When they used it this time, I arrested on them. I heard the radiologist who was working on me go over to the telephone, and I heard very clearly as he dialed it. I heard him say, 'Dr. James, I've killed your patient, Mrs. Martin.' And I knew I wasn't dead. I tried to move or to let them know, but I couldn't. When they were trying to resuscitate me, I could hear them telling how many cc's of something to give me, but I didn't feel the needles going in." Almost everyone who reports hearing of his or her death tries in vain to deny it. The person can see and hear and think but is unable to move or speak.

Feelings of serenity. For those studied, the early stages of an NDE often involve extremely pleasant feelings and sensations. Any pain that the person may have been feeling has disappeared. After one man received a severe head injury, his vital signs were undetectable. He said later: "At the point of injury there was a momentary flash of pain, but then all the pain vanished. I had the feeling of floating in a dark space. The day was bitterly cold, yet while I was in that blackness all I felt was warmth and the most extreme comfort I have ever experienced . . . . I remember thinking, 'I must be dead.' "

Noise. Those experiencing NDEs often hear unusual sounds, sometimes of a very unpleasant nature. A man who "died" for twenty minutes during an abdominal operation reported "a really bad buzzing noise coming from inside my head. It made me very uncomfortable." On the other hand, the sound can be magnificent. A young woman who had suffered from internal bleeding said that at the instant she collapsed she "began to hear music of some sort, a majestic, really beautiful sort of music."

The dark tunnel. As they hear the noise, many subjects report the sensation of being pulled rapidly through a dark tunnel, valley, cave, well, cylinder, or other elongated space. One informant stopped breathing because of an allergic reaction to a local anesthetic: "The first thing that happened—it was real quick—was that I went through this dark, black vacuum at super speed. You could compare it to a tunnel, I guess. I felt like I was riding on a roller coaster train at an amusement park, going through this tunnel at a tremendous speed."

Leaving the body. Often what people find to be the most surprising and affecting part of the near-death experience is an apparent out-of-body episode. This awareness of separation from one's body frequently follows the trip through the dark tunnel.

One woman who underwent such an experience recalled: "I was admitted to the hospital with heart trouble, and the next morning, lying in the hospital bed, I began to have a very severe pain in my chest. I pushed the button beside the bed to call for the nurses, and they came in and started working on me. I was quite uncomfortable lying on my back so I turned over, and as I did I quit breathing and my heart stopped beating. Just then, I heard the nurses shout, 'Code pink! Code pink!' As they were saying this, I could feel myself moving out of my body and sliding down between the mattress and the rail on the side of the bed— actually it seemed as if I went *through* the rail—on down to the floor. Then I started rising upward, slowly. On my way up, I saw more nurses come running into the room—there must have been a dozen of them . . . . I drifted on up past the light fixture—I saw it from the side and very distinctly— and then I stopped, floating right below the ceiling, looking down. I felt almost as though I were a piece of paper that someone had blown up to the ceiling."

Meeting others. Spirits of dead relatives, friends, or guardian beings seem to appear in order to ease the loneliness of the transition into death. A woman who underwent a very difficult childbirth heard the doctor tell her relatives that she was dying. "Even as I heard him saying this I felt myself coming to," she recounted. "As I did, I realized that all these people were there, almost in multitudes it seems, hovering around the ceiling of the room. They were all people I had known in my past life, but who had passed on before. I recognized my grandmother and a girl I had known when I was in school, and many other relatives and friends. It seems that I mainly saw their faces and felt their

presence. They all seemed pleased. It was a very happy occasion, and I felt that they had come to protect or to guide me. It was almost as if I were coming home."

The being of light. Possibly the most amazing element in the accounts that Moody studied, and the one that has the most profound effect on the individual, is the encounter with the being of light. Typically, the light is dim at first but then waxes brighter and brighter until it reaches an unearthly or indescribable brilliance. At the same time, those who have seen the light say that it does not hurt their eyes or keep them from being able to see other things. Perhaps, Moody notes, this is because the dying do not have physical eyes to be dazzled.

In every case that Moody recorded, those who saw the light as part of a near-death experience knew that it was a being, one who emanated love and warmth beyond description. The identification of this being varies with the religious background of the dying person. Most Christians see the light as Christ, whereas Jews have identified it as an angel. The being may communicate with the dying person, seemingly by thought transference. Usually it asks a question that is understood as "Are you prepared to die?" or "What have you done with your life to show me?" or "Is it worth it?" None of the subjects felt that the questions were judgmental or condemning.

One person remembered the experience this way: "It was just a tremendous amount of light . . . . I just can't describe it. It seemed that it covered everything . . . . At first, when the light came, I wasn't sure what was happening, but then, it asked, it kind of asked me if I was ready to die. It was like talking to a person, but a person wasn't there. The light's what was talking to me, but in a *voice.* Now, I think that the voice that was talking to me actually realized that I wasn't ready to die. You know, it was just kind of testing me more than anything else. Yet, from the moment the light spoke to me, I felt really good—secure and loved."

The review. The appearance of the being of light and his probing questions may precede a moment of startling intensity during which the being presents the person with an overview of his or her life. The review is very fast, like a movie shown at high speed, although some respondents said that they saw everything at once and were able to take it all in at a glance.

One woman recalled her experience: "When the light appeared, the first thing he said to me was 'What do you have to show me that you've done with your life?' or something to this effect. And that's when these flashbacks started. I thought, 'Gee, what is going on?' because all of a sudden, I was back early in my childhood. And from then on, it was like I was walking from the time of my very early life, on through each year of my life, right up to the present."

The border. In a few cases, people feel themselves approaching a border or limit of some kind. It has been described as a door, a fence, a body of water, a gray mist, or simply a line. They may see the border as the threshold between life and death. A man dying of kidney disease first saw the being of light. Next, the "thoughts or words came into my mind: 'Do you want to die?' And I replied that I didn't know since I knew nothing about death. Then the white light said, 'Come over this line and you will learn.' "

Coming back. Obviously, the people that Raymond Moody talked with had come back from the apparent threshold of death, or there would have been no material for *Life after Life.* The return represents an important element in the near-death experience. It comes at the end of the experience and at a time when many of the dying have lost any desire to reenter their bodies. Once a dying person reaches a certain depth in the experience, respondents have said, he or she rarely wants to return. This is especially true for those who go so far into an NDE that they encounter the being of light.

Several mothers of young children said they would have preferred to stay in the spiritual world but felt an obligation to go back and raise their children. Others said they returned because of unfinished tasks on earth.

Coming back quite often involves another trip through the dark tunnel, though few of Moody's respondents experienced an actual reentry into their physical bodies. Most

Some people who relate near-death experiences describe a walk through a lush valley, deep and dark but ove

...helmingly peaceful. A bright light beckons from the far side, and a luminous guide may lead the spirit onward.

said they simply lapsed into unconsciousness at the end of the experience and woke later to find themselves back in their flesh-and-blood bodies.

Moody named four other characteristic elements of NDEs, all of which could fall under the heading "beginning again": telling others, corroboration of the experience, changed lives, and new views of death. People who undergo near-death experiences have no doubts about the reality and importance of their NDEs, says Moody, but few are willing to discuss them openly. They usually find that a skeptical society is simply not ready to receive NDE reports with sympathy and understanding. One survivor commented, "I tried to tell my minister, but he told me I had been hallucinating, so I shut up."

Because of the difficulty of communicating what may be the most profound experience in their lives, people who have had an NDE may believe they are unique. Moody found that many of his subjects were greatly relieved to hear that other people had had similar experiences. All felt that the experience had changed them. "In other words," said one survivor, "there's more to life than Friday night movies and the football game. And there's more to me that I don't even know about. And then I started thinking about 'What is the limit of the human and of the mind?' It just opened me up to a whole new world."

Finally, Moody found that the near-death experience almost always alters one's attitude toward death, especially for those who before their NDE thought that death meant complete extinction—of the spirit as well as the body. According to one person, "Some people I have known are so afraid, so scared. I always smile to myself when I hear people doubt that there is an afterlife, or say, 'When you're dead, you're gone.' I think to myself, 'They really don't know.' "

Few of Moody's respondents had experiences containing all of these elements. And for some, the NDE was even unpleasant. One woman remarked, "If you leave here a tormented soul, you will be a tormented soul over there, too." A widower who tried to commit suicide said, "I didn't go where [my wife] was. I went to an awful place . . . . I immediately saw what a mistake I had made." Such cases were a small minority of Moody's sample, however.

The publication in 1977 of Moody's second book, *Reflections on Life after Life,* which backed up the conclusions of the first book with more case histories, marked the end of the first phase of near-death studies. Characterized by informal, anecdotal studies aimed at a popular audience, with little concern for documentation or systematic analysis, this period nevertheless moved a number of scientists to begin more rigorous NDE research.

In November 1977, Raymond Moody and a number of other independent researchers met in Charlottesville, Virginia, to discuss new avenues for NDE research. As a result, the Association for the Scientific Study of Near-Death Phenomena, which included most of the professionals who were active in the emerging field of NDE studies, sprang into being the following year. Over the next few years, articles on near-death experiences began to appear in the medical, psychological, and philosophical literature. Doctors read papers on the subject at professional meetings, and religious scholars began to add their commentary.

Moody's work inspired the next major study of NDEs, a survey conducted by Connecticut psychologist Kenneth Ring. Ring, who had previously studied altered states of consciousness, spent thirteen months interviewing people who had come close to death. In 1980 he published *Life at Death,* the first book to apply statistical methods to the analysis of near-death-experience reports.

Ring's research, which analyzed NDEs with graphs and statistical tables, substantiated Moody's description of the near-death core experience. The psychologist wanted to delve further into the issue, however, asking questions such as: How common are the details outlined by Moody? Does it make a difference how one dies (or comes close to death)? What is the connection between religious sentiment and the near-death experience? And what changes occur in the survivor's subsequent life?

Acknowledging that his samples were not entirely

random, Ring found that near-death experiences were reported by 48 percent of those who had come close to dying. However, given the sampling problem, all he would really commit to saying was that such experiences were not rare. The way in which a person approached death—through illness, accident, or suicide—seemed not to have a significant effect on the experience. Nor did depth of religious belief: Religious and nonreligious people had NDEs in about the same numbers, and the nature of their beliefs did not affect the character of their NDEs, although it did change the interpretation of them. Frequently, near-death experiences made people more religious than they had been previously. Ring's research agreed with Moody's in finding that survivors believed they had received an important new start in life. Predictably, they also had a much stronger belief in an afterlife and less fear of death.

Ring concedes that his studies will hardly prove the existence of life after death. He does offer up his own beliefs on the subject: "I *do* believe—but not just on the basis of my own or others' data regarding near-death experiences—that we continue to have a conscious existence after our physical death and that the core experience does represent its beginning, a glimpse of things to come. I am, in fact, convinced—both from my own personal experiences and from my studies as a psychologist—that it is possible to become conscious of 'other realities' and that the coming close to death represents one avenue to a higher 'frequency domain,' or reality, which will be fully accessible to us following what we call death."

Finally, Ring speculates "with considerable intellectual reluctance" that the being of light and the voice that seems to be heard by thought transference in the NDE come from within—from a "higher self" that he suggests is vastly different from normal consciousness. The higher self, says Ring, could have total knowledge of the individual and could produce a review of his or her life in total detail.

Although Kenneth Ring refuses to use the word soul because of its religious connotations, he ends by saying that the feeling of being with God can be explained by a rather traditional philosophic view. "If one can accept the idea of a higher self," says the psychologist, "it is not difficult to assume that that self—as well as the individual himself—is actually an aspect of God, or the Creator, or any such term with which one feels comfortable."

Ring's initial observations on the widespread nature of NDEs were confirmed in 1982, when Atlanta cardiologist Michael B. Sabom published a book titled *Recollections of Death*. Interestingly, Sabom began his studies a strong skeptic about NDEs but became convinced of their reality during five years of research on the subject. Sabom had first heard of NDEs in 1976 during an adult Sunday school class he attended in Gainesville, Florida. Participants in the class were discussing Raymond Moody's book *Life after Life*.

Asked for his opinion, Dr. Sabom recalls that the kindest thing he could think of to say at the moment was, "I don't believe it." Nevertheless, later the same week, he found himself agreeing to participate in a presentation of the Moody book to a churchwide audience. The doctor was to field any medical questions that came up. In preparation, he decided to interview patients in the local hospital to see if he could find anyone who had had an NDE. He soon found a woman who described her experience to him. "To my utter amazement," writes Sabom, "the details matched the descriptions in *Life after Life*. I was even more impressed by her sincerity and the deep personal significance her experience had had for her."

Sabom had been skeptical because he had never heard of such an experience, either from patients of his own or from his colleagues. Most doctors were inclined to be doubtful of the phenomenon, reacting partly to the somewhat sensational media coverage touched off by the success of Moody's *Life after Life* and the lectures of Elisabeth Kübler-Ross. Near-death experiences had become the stuff of TV talk shows, checkout-counter tabloids, a quasi-documentary movie, and even weekly contests for the best out-of-body experience. Sabom said that his preresearch views were best expressed on the pages of a 1979 article in

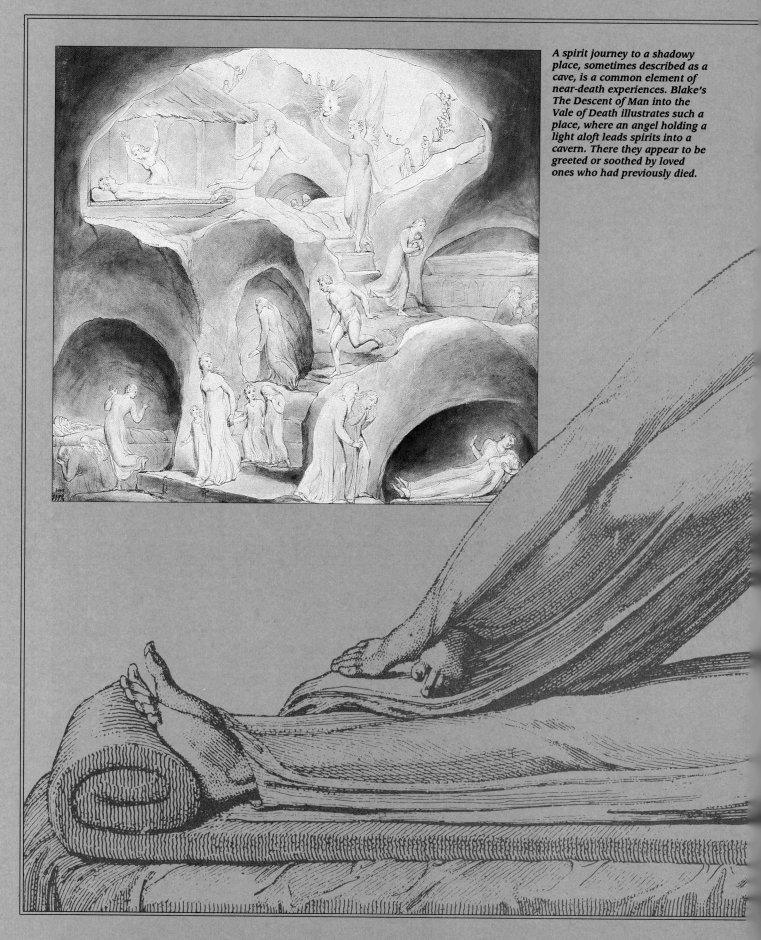

A spirit journey to a shadowy place, sometimes described as a cave, is a common element of near-death experiences. Blake's *The Descent of Man into the Vale of Death* illustrates such a place, where an angel holding a light aloft leads spirits into a cavern. There they appear to be greeted or soothed by loved ones who had previously died.

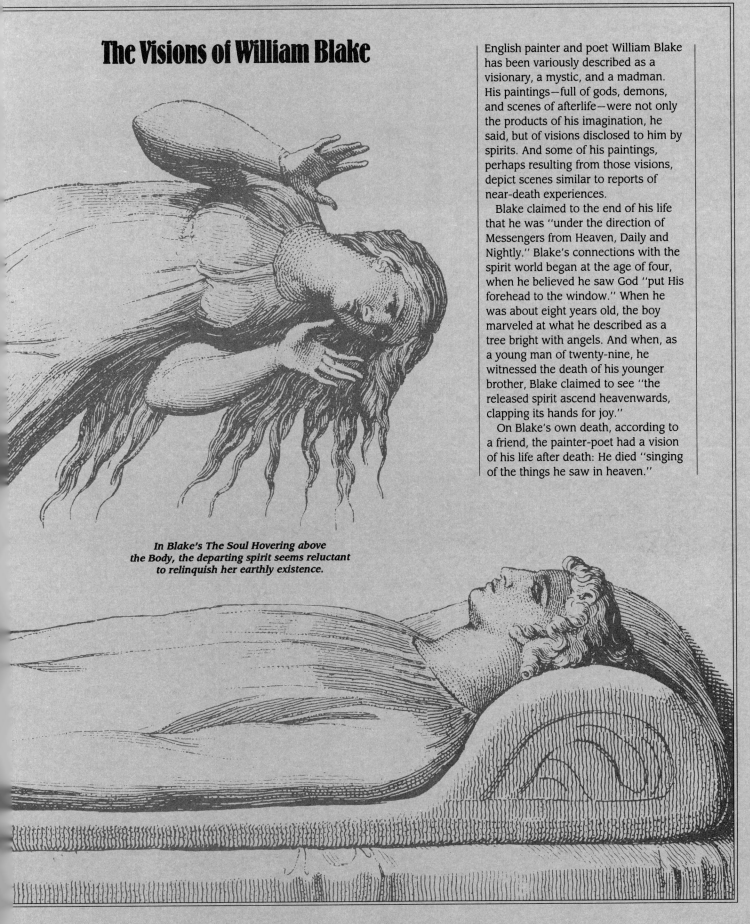

The Visions of William Blake

English painter and poet William Blake has been variously described as a visionary, a mystic, and a madman. His paintings—full of gods, demons, and scenes of afterlife—were not only the products of his imagination, he said, but of visions disclosed to him by spirits. And some of his paintings, perhaps resulting from those visions, depict scenes similar to reports of near-death experiences.

Blake claimed to the end of his life that he was "under the direction of Messengers from Heaven, Daily and Nightly." Blake's connections with the spirit world began at the age of four, when he believed he saw God "put His forehead to the window." When he was about eight years old, the boy marveled at what he described as a tree bright with angels. And when, as a young man of twenty-nine, he witnessed the death of his younger brother, Blake claimed to see "the released spirit ascend heavenwards, clapping its hands for joy."

On Blake's own death, according to a friend, the painter-poet had a vision of his life after death: He died "singing of the things he saw in heaven."

In Blake's The Soul Hovering above the Body, the departing spirit seems reluctant to relinquish her earthly existence.

Angelic figures line a radiant staircase spiraling toward heaven in William Blake's watercolor Jacob's Dream. As in many reported near-death experiences, the angels appear to be leading spirits—some of them children—toward a comforting light. Other angels are descending the staircase, perhaps to summon new spirits to the next realm.

the *Journal of the American Medical Association* that stated, "People who undergo these 'death experiences' are suffering from a hypoxic [oxygen-deficient] state, during which they try to deal psychologically with the anxieties provoked by medical procedures and talk . . . . We are dealing here with the fantasy of death . . . . Five years and 116 interviews later," Sabom said, "I am convinced that my original suspicions about this were wrong."

Determined to be objective in his research, Sabom interviewed subjects in such a way that they were not at first aware of his real interest. He did not limit himself to those who claimed to have had an NDE but questioned a random sample of patients who had suffered near-fatal medical crises. He found that 43 percent had vivid memories of their brush with death, one-third of them had out-of-body experiences, and about half recalled traveling through a dark tunnel toward a bright light.

Sabom examined alternate explanations for NDEs: that they are simply lies, dreams, hallucinations, or drug-induced delusions, or are caused by drastic changes in the brain just prior to death. In his opinion, none of these explanations adequately accounts for the near-death experience. For instance, some of his patients could accurately report the details of resuscitation efforts that occurred while they were believed to be unconscious, details that could not be duplicated by a control group of medically experienced people who were asked to guess at such procedures.

After considering alternatives, Sabom did feel that the out-of-body experience is probably authentic and that during the time when mind and body are separated, a person can make accurate observations and enter into a mystical state. He is cautious about his conclusions, however. "Personally, I believe in life after death," he said. "But I do not believe the work I have done proves life after death."

At about the same time that Sabom published his book, Kenneth Ring became the head of the newly founded International Association for Near Death Studies (IANDS) at the University of Connecticut. And in 1984 he published a sequel to *Life at Death,* a book called *Heading toward Ome-ga,* in which the psychologist pushes his speculations on NDEs even further. While writing his second book, Ring received a moving letter from a young woman who claimed to have had a life-changing experience, containing many of the elements of an NDE, without having been near death or even sick. Her letter was not unique. Ring says that there are more than a hundred like it in IANDS's files, missives from people who said they had had "what you call a near-death experience" during meditation, childbirth, a personal crisis, or a church service, or spontaneously.

"What occurs during an NDE," Ring decided, "has nothing inherently to do with death or with the transition into death." He goes on to suggest that the NDE should be considered one of a family of related mystical experiences, similar to some Indian forms of enlightenment. Overall, Ring's highly provocative and rather daring proposal is that the NDE itself might just be an evolutionary mechanism for moving individuals into the next stage of human development. Perhaps, he suggests, such occurrences unlock previously dormant spiritual potential and help to produce a higher mode of consciousness.

Ring observes that there are no systematic studies of the incidence of such transcendental experiences. Nevertheless, as he points out, a 1982 Gallup poll of NDEs concluded that one in twenty Americans has had a near-death experience. "Obviously," says Ring, "the thousands of NDErs who have been interviewed are speaking for millions of their silent brethren."

As NDE research continues, so too does the debate. The phenomenon itself is widely accepted as real—almost no one questions that people are honestly reporting their experiences—but its meaning is still controversial. Despite a century of active investigation, the crucial issue remains very much as it was in the 1880s: Do NDEs prove the existence of life after death? Or is there a psychological or physiological explanation for them?

Skeptics raise a number of objections to a survivalist

interpretation of NDEs. For instance, most people who have been close to death simply do not have NDEs. Some return with nightmarish experiences. Moreover, the primary Moody-type NDE sometimes happens to people who are not in danger of death at all, so the experience could not always be related to dying. And finally, the evidence for NDEs comes only from the living. "Clinically dead" is an ambiguous term often used by those who tell of such experiences, but the fact is that the person did not really die. For obvious reasons, there is no evidence about what happens to people who actually die.

Nonsurvivalist explanations for near-death experiences generally fall into two camps: One, NDEs are psychological constructs, illusions triggered by the stressful occasion of approaching death, or two, NDEs are hallucinations produced by chemical changes in the dying brain. The depersonalization theory of Russell Noyes is one such psychological explanation, although even Noyes admits that it does not cover all facets of mystical consciousness. Some observers have also suggested that the near-death experience is an archetype, a kind of universal myth stored in everyone's unconscious mind and brought forth only in extreme situations. Others prefer a physiological explanation, noting similarities between near-death experiences and drug-induced hallucinations. (For instance, LSD visions often include a trip through a tunnel.) Perhaps, they say, hospital anesthesia could account for such experiences. Or, it is possible that the overstressed brain is itself suffering a chemical disorder or reacting to oxygen deprivation (common in dying people), which might cause vivid visions.

Clearly, near-death experiences remain an enigma, and as such they have spawned an entire field of study. As of 1986, at least forty scholars and researchers in the United States alone were active in near-death research. IANDS publishes *Anabiosis,* a scholarly journal on the subject. Psychology and psychiatry textbooks describe NDE research. Graduate students have written doctoral theses on the subject.

Meanwhile, study in the area continues along more specialized lines than in the past. Researchers are currently conducting cross-cultural surveys to see if the NDE is truly a universal phenomenon, and they are examining the experiences of specialized populations such as children, the blind, and prisoners. Doctors have designed neurophysiological experiments to assess the possible role of endorphins (hormones that act on the nervous system to reduce pain) and other natural chemicals in NDEs.

The accumulated knowledge about near-death experiences seems to have some practical applications. Apparently, simple exposure to NDE findings tends to reduce almost everyone's fear of death and dying. Nurses, therapists, clergy, social workers, and funeral directors use their knowledge of near-death experiences to help lessen such fears in hospitals, nursing homes, and hospices.

Near-death research continues to surprise. For example, a 1986 paper on the psychoanalysis of nineteen NDE survivors reported that they came to treatment already having the ability to free associate—to allow the mind to wander freely without any blocks or hesitancy. David Raft, the psychiatrist who wrote the study, claimed that free association is usually possible only after years of successful analysis or for "a spiritual adept who has mastered the discipline of religious contemplation."

Philosophers have wrangled for centuries over such questions as the so-called mind-body problem, which asks how it is possible for an invisible, immaterial mind to relate to a visible, material body. Perhaps when all the varieties of the out-of-body experience are better understood, the philosophers will agree on a solution.

Until then, investigators will have to live with the kind of fascinated frustration expressed by cardiologist Sabom. Many of the patients in his study have died since he interviewed them. "I just wonder when I go back and listen to the tape," says Sabom, "if they found that what happened in the near-death experience is what actually happens in death. It's an eerie feeling to know that now they know, and I'm still here wondering."

Back from the Brink

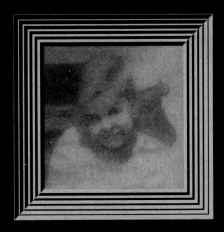

Students of the near-death experience say that no two people who have had one describe the sojourn in precisely the same way. Still, those NDE stories that have been reported are remarkably similar in many ways, no matter what the age, sex, social station, or religious beliefs of the teller—and regardless of the cause of "death." The details may vary in order, and they are by no means common to each experience, yet a pattern does emerge from them.

Overall, the pattern is most notable for contradicting the notion that death is fearsome, dreadful, and final. Those who have skirted the precipice say that, on the contrary, death is no more than a pleasant and peaceful passage to a realm sublime beyond description. What exists in the next world, it seems, has only the dimmest analogs in this one. To die is to awake to colors, shapes, and sounds that beggar common words because they lie outside of common perception.

Some researchers contend the NDE affords those special few who have them a tantalizing glimpse of a transcendent state that awaits all of us after death. Others believe it is merely an example of the indomitable human mind at work, fabricating a dazzling exit from the only reality we will ever know. Whatever else they may be, the near-death experiences that have been studied are impressively consistent. The accounts may vary in particulars, but they seldom stray from certain central themes. The following pages illustrate guideposts of a common NDE.

Here a traffic accident has brought a victim close to death, or perhaps he has actually died. Even so, he is aware of his situation; his powers of perception are somehow intact. Yet he feels detached from his physical body, a spectator at his own death. He is calm and peaceful. There is no pain or fear. He becomes aware of a dark space, a tunnel, and he feels himself drifting through it. The sensation is nothing but pleasant and comforting.

At the end of the tunnel the victim sees friends and relatives who have already died. He understands that they are there to help him through his transition from life to death. Then he sees a light, at first dim, but quickly growing ineffably clear, brilliant, and compelling. He senses within the light a being who may seem somehow to be the light itself, a being that projects an unconditional and enveloping love.

The dying person understands that the being wants him to review his life. No judgment or condemnation is implied. The person remains suffused with feelings of love and acceptance as before him appear shifting scenes that are the sum and essence of his life's experiences and thoughts. The process is at once both instantaneous and timeless, and it implies a choice: He may die, or he may return to complete some unfinished facet of his life.

Retracing his voyage through the tunnel, the accident victim finds himself back in his physical body. He is aware of people trying to revive him. He has not died after all, but his life has been fundamentally altered. Hereafter he is not likely to fear death as he once may have. At the same time, he may have a heightened appreciation for life and possibly a sense of spiritual values underlying the material world.

Exploring Past Incarnations

A young woman visits a psychotherapist, complaining of claustrophobia; in the session she suddenly sees herself trapped in the hold of a slave ship. A man with incapacitating headaches recounts, under hypnosis, an earlier existence that ended when he died of a brain tumor. A writer unable to finish her books becomes convinced of a previous incarnation in colonial America, where she was prosecuted for heresy.

These people and others throughout the world believe that the answers to their problems may lie in the past—not the traditional past of childhood memories, but the past of a previous life. Exploring these lives with them are an increasing number of counselors and psychologists who specialize in what they call past-life or regression therapy. Patients undergoing such treatment are encouraged to think back to a time before they were born and to trace links between that supposed existence and their current life.

One such counselor is Dr. Garrett Oppenheim, who is a psychotherapist in Tappan, New York. Oppenheim does not claim to have proven the reality of reincarnation. He does contend that in visualizing these scenes, whatever their source and however fragmentary and unverifiable they may be, his clients will better understand the forces that control their lives. Client Monica (her real name withheld for privacy) agrees. In 1986, she attended Oppenheim's lectures on past-life regression, and soon began consulting him privately. She believes that under hypnosis she has discovered a previous existence as a man in the American southwest. Her story, told in her own words, is represented with period photographs on the next six pages.

Hypnotized, yet aware of her surroundings in psychotherapist Garrett Oppenheim's office, Monica watches scenes that seem to depict an earlier life passing before her eyes like a vivid movie.

My name in that life was John Ralph Wainwright. I don't remember my earliest years in that existence, but I do know that I grew up on a ranch outside of the town of Wisconsin, Arizona, in the late nineteenth century. The ranch had three buildings and a big house with a lot of mullioned windows. My parents were hard-working, but well-off—my father was a well-known horsetrader.

I know I had brothers and sisters, but I wasn't able to identify how many, or who they were. I went back to a scene at a dinner table and there were lots of kids there, but maybe some of them were the children of ranch hands. I usually go back to scenes that are focal points in that earlier life, that have people who are also in this life. I guess my brothers and sisters in that life weren't important to the life I'm in now.

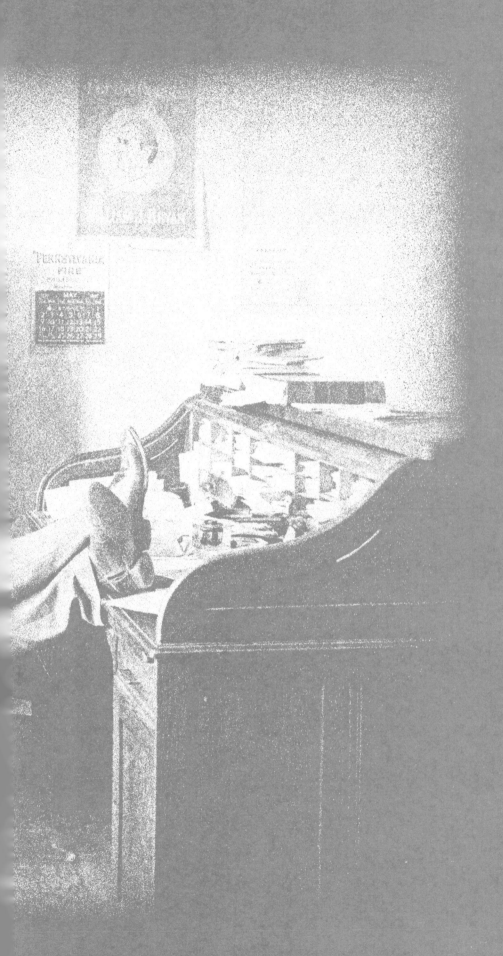

When I was a young man I became a deputy sheriff. I liked that job because I could be outdoors a lot, not sitting at a desk—which is still the case in this life; I don't like being confined.

Eventually I married a bank president's daughter, Lu-Anne Simmons, and worked at the Wiscon Valley Bank. I didn't like that job at all, so after a few years I went back to the sheriff's office and was promoted. I remember that I hated to wear hats, so when I had to wear one with my uniform, I pushed it back on my head. That's why I was known as "the sheriff without a hat." I'm like that today; I can't bear to have anything on my head.

I died on July 7, 1907. I know the date exactly because when I went back to the scene under hypnosis I looked at the calendar on the desk. It was a Sunday, I think, and I went into the office to do some paperwork, taking my son Joshua with me. I was sitting there thinking about how happy I was with my life right then, when three men burst into the room with their guns drawn. I don't remember who they were; maybe they were men I had sent to jail. I leaped up, and one of them shot me. It's funny, when I go back to that scene, I hear the shots hit me, but I don't feel any pain.

The way I died then, just when I was feeling happy, may be why in my current life I've unconsciously avoided the things that might contribute to my happiness. I think I've worked that out now.

I was reborn in 1943.

CHAPTER 3

Stepping into New Lives

he little boy called Sujith had not yet reached his second birthday in 1971 when, according to his family, he began to talk about an earlier life. Expressing himself in the limited speech of a child so young, adding sounds and gestures when vocabulary failed, Sujith said that his name in his past life had been Sammy and that he had been a railroad worker and later a seller of bootleg arrack, a potent liquor distilled from rice, molasses, or other ingredients. He said that as Sammy he had lived in the village of Gorakana, about eight miles south of his present home in the suburbs of Colombo, Sri Lanka (formerly Ceylon). He went on to relate that his—or Sammy's—wife was named Maggie and that one day, when he was drunk and they had quarreled, he had set out on foot along the busy highway in front of their house, only to be struck and killed by a passing truck. Repeatedly, the toddler demanded to be taken to Gorakana. He also had a precocious taste for cigarettes and arrack.

Sujith's mother, Nandanie, who had been divorced from the boy's father soon after the child's birth, was not entirely mystified by such behavior. She and the other members of her family knew no one in Gorakana, nor did they know if a bootlegger named Sammy had ever existed. But like most Sri Lankans, they were Buddhists and accepted the idea of reincarnation, which holds that every human has a soul or psychic essence separate from the physical self, and that this psychic entity survives death to reappear, usually anonymously, in another body at some later time. The fact that little Sujith might contain the spirit of a quarrelsome drunkard from a neighboring town and be able to give witness to it was hardly unimaginable. Thus Nandanie expressed no objection when a monk in a nearby temple, having heard about the boy, asked if he could investigate.

The monk interviewed Sujith at length, wrote down significant details of his story, and selected sixteen items about his past life that could be checked for accuracy. He then visited Gorakana on several occasions and managed to verify nearly all of them. He discovered, for example, that a man named Sammy Fernando had lived in Gorakana until six months before Sujith's birth. This Sammy had been a former railway worker and an arrack dealer. He also had a wife named Maggie and a father named Jamis. People in Gorakana confirmed that Sammy Fernando had been killed by a truck outside his home shortly after quarreling with his wife; the dead man was, they added, a hard-drinking, violent, and impulsively generous man who had had repeated brushes with the police. He was a cigarette smoker.

It was not long before a newspaper article about Sujith found its way to Ian Stevenson, a professor of psychiatry at the University of Virginia and director of the division of personality studies at the university medical center. Since the early 1960s, Stevenson has become the preeminent scientific researcher studying cases of purported reincarnation, or metempsychosis, as it is sometimes called. A low-key, publicity-shunning figure in a field that has many showy personalities among its population, he has quietly been accumulating a vast and extraordinary file of reincarnation cases. The total now exceeds 2,000.

When Stevenson gets wind of a potentially good case, he does not just investigate it—he lays siege. He travels to the subject's home, wherever it may be, and to the place where the person allegedly lived in the past. (He covered an average of 55,000 miles a year between 1966 and 1977.) Stevenson conducts dozens of tape-recorded interviews, which are often supplemented by follow-up visits years later. His fact-finding technique, he says, combines the approaches of a lawyer, a psychiatrist, a historian, and a detective—he has even used a polygraph test on occasion.

Stevenson gave the Sujith/ Sammy case the usual thorough attention. The psychiatrist traveled to Sri Lanka in 1973 and conducted a series of interviews with everyone involved, including Sujith, who was by

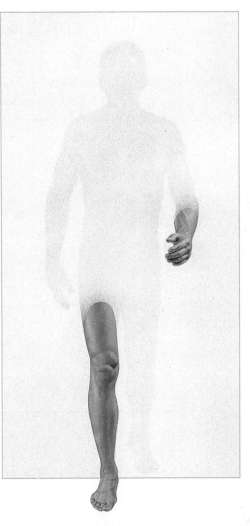

then three-and-one-half years old, and Sammy's widow, Maggilin Fernando. In so doing, he was able to find corroboration for fifty-nine of Sujith's statements about his earlier life. Stevenson discovered additional behavior parallels between the child and the person whose life he claimed to remember—including a taste for spicy food and a preference for wearing a certain type of shirt and sarong not commonly found among young children. Both persons shared an enthusiasm for singing, used profanity freely, were given to physical violence, and were notably generous with their meager possessions. The toddler even displayed a peculiar wariness around policemen and a pronounced fear of trucks that seemed to have parallels in Sammy's life. Sujith also showed what seemed to be instant recognition of a number of people in Sammy's family when they were brought together. He called Maggilin "Maggie" and other pet names that Sammy used, and made her cry by proclaiming "I love you Maggie" and then blaming her for his death.

Stevenson's fieldwork turned up no evidence that Sujith's family and the Fernandos had previously known each other. The closest connection was a former drinking companion of Sammy's who was casually acquainted with Sujith's family, but both this man and Sujith's mother and grandmother denied ever having discussed Sammy. Likewise, Sujith's eccentric behavior and his easy recognition of Sammy's relatives seemed to rule out the possibility that the child was pretending or fantasizing, or that anyone else was using him as part of an elaborate deception, even assuming that he could memorize all the facts he seemed to know at ages two and three. The only other explanation, from Stevenson's vantage, was reincarnation. Calling it "one of the strongest known to me," he included

Sujith's story in the second volume of a series he titled Cases of the Reincarnation Type.

Only recently has reincarnation been subjected to any sort of systematic study. But the possibility of multiple lives has been accepted on faith since ancient times. Indeed, belief in reincarnation may date back to the Stone Age, some 12,000 years ago or earlier. Archaeologists, noting that it was common practice at the time to bury the dead in the fetal position, have speculated that prehistoric peoples may have been preparing the bodies for a literal rebirth of the spirit. And the phenomenon of reincarnation has played—and continues to play—a part in countless primitive cultures around the world, among peoples who were and are living in remote regions of Africa, Asia, Australia, and the Americas.

Reincarnation has also been incorporated into the formal beliefs of more civilized cultures, extending back as far as the beginnings of recorded history. The ancient Egyptians, for example, enclosed in the coffins of their dead texts that attested to the deceased's virtues, in the hopes of persuading the god Osiris to grant them further lives. Herodotus, the Greek historian who wrote extensively on Egyptian customs, reported that Egyptians believed that it took 3,000 years for a spirit to complete the full cycle of lives through which it had to go.

And reincarnation figured in the teachings of many ancient Greek philosopher-mystics. Pythagoras, the sixth-century B.C. mathematician and mystic, claimed to have lived many other lives, including that of a Trojan warrior, a prophet, a peasant, a prostitute, and a shopkeeper. Once, he reportedly stopped a man from beating a puppy, saying: "Do not hit him, it is the soul of a friend of mine. I recognized it when I heard it cry out." Plato, the fifth-century B.C. sage, was fully persuaded of reincarnation, and he offered a theory on how the soul gradually ascends (or descends) through nine degrees of righteousness in a series of rebirth experiences. Describing the process in the *Phaedrus,* he depicted the lowest rank as that of tyrants and others of extreme unrighteousness. However, he said, those who live righteously gradually journey upward to ever higher levels, the soul eventually entering the body of a gymnast or physician (fourth rank), a politician or economist (third rank), and a righteous king or warrior (second level). Finally, when the soul has shown itself worthy of true enlightenment and is divorced completely from subservience to the material world, it may be born into the body of a philosopher, artist, musician, or lover. Only then, according to Plato, is the soul ready to cease its rebirth and find unending peace in a heavenly realm of sublime knowledge.

The classical version of reincarnation had a subversive influence on early Christian thought. Then, as now, the idea of rebirth was regarded by most churchmen as hereti-

This eighteenth-century painting depicts the god Vishnu in his incarnation as the white horse Kalki. The Hindu doctrine of transmigration holds that souls must travel through various lives, animal and human, before achieving union with the Brahma, the all-encompassing divine principle. Each rebirth is governed by karma, the sum of one's thoughts and actions in the previous life.

cal; orthodox Christian doctrine, after all, declares that the souls of the departed pass directly to heaven, hell, or purgatory, and not into another physical being.

Notable among Christians with differing views was Origen, a second-century philosopher from Alexandria, Egypt. Origen devoted his life to writing and teaching a kind of neoplatonic Christianity that included belief in reincarnation. In one of the few fragments of his writing that has survived, he described how he understood rebirth to work: "Everyone, therefore, of those who descend to the earth is, according to his deserts or to the position that he had there, ordained to be born in this world either in a different place, or in a different nation, or in a different occupation, or with different infirmities, or to be descended from religious or at least less pious parents; so as sometimes to bring about that an Israelite descends among the Scythians, and a poor Egyptian is brought down to Judaea."

Origen was posthumously condemned for such "blasphemous opinions" by Pope Anastasius in 400. But his influence lingered on with sufficient power that the sixth-century Council of Constantinople issued a decree of anathema against him and all who accepted his concept of "monstrous restoration."

Apparently, the council's reach did not extend very far. By the eleventh century a diverse collection of some seventy or more heretical sects, many of them stressing reincarnation, were flourishing throughout Christendom. Perhaps the most influential was a group of dissidents known as the Albigenses (for the French town of Albi) or Cathars ("purified ones"), who believed that human souls were fallen spirits for whom a human incarnation was a period of probation and expiation. Good lives were rewarded with rebirth into a body capable of still greater spiritual development. Bad lives could only lead to rebirth into a body full of pain, suffering, and still more evil. The Cathars, who also would tolerate little of this world, including music, papal wealth, and the high standard of living of much of the clergy, ultimately were put down by the Church *(pages 100-101),* and reincarnation was once again declared outside of Christian doctrine.

In the East, the concept of reincarnation can also be traced to ancient times—and it has remained a central tenet of mainstream religious beliefs and practices. It was probably first articulated in a formal sense in the Upanishads, the concluding section of a vast body of traditional hymns or vedas preserved by the high priests of the Aryan peoples who invaded India sometime around 1500 B.C. According to the Upanishads, the individual ego or spirit *(atman)* has its origin in a transcendent spiritual essence. The atman begins its existence in an immature state, and in order to grow in wisdom and reach spiritual maturity, it must undergo an endless cycle of rebirth, suffering, and death. With each

French illustrator Émile Bayard depicts the fiery martyrdom of the Cathars at the Inquisition's hands in this nineteenth-century woodcut.

The Return of the Martyred Cathars

In medieval France there flourished a Christian sect that believed in reincarnation, as well as in the dualism of spiritual and physical, good and evil. Its members were known as Albigenses, after the town of Albi, or, as they preferred, Cathari—"purified ones." The Cathars were an irritant to the Roman Catholic Church, which deemed them both heretical and a threat to churchly power. After a long struggle, the Catholics conquered the Cathar stronghold of Montségur in the French Pyrenees. Two hundred ten Cathars captured there refused to renounce their faith, and in 1244 they were burned at the stake in Toulouse.

To an Oxford-educated English psychiatrist named Arthur Guirdham, this was familiar history and no more—until a young woman came to him in 1962 complaining of terrifying nightmares. During the next four years, "Mrs. Smith," as Guirdham called her, poured forth a torrent of mental torments, many centering on alleged memories of living among the Cathars in thirteenth-century France. As a schoolgirl she had imagined a Cathar lover named Roger, and on her school books she wrote bits of Provençal poetry he had recited to her.

The fortified chateau of Montségur in the Pyrenean foothills seemed an impregnable Cathar stronghold until the Catholics besieged it in 1243-44.

Her story struck some resonant chord in the psychiatrist, and, checking on fragments of Cathar history, Guirdham found her stories uncannily accurate. She said, for instance, that the Cathars wore dark blue robes.

Guirdham knew that traditional historians recorded the robes as being black, but consulting an expert, he learned that new research confirmed they were indeed dark blue.

In time, Guirdham came to believe he himself was the reincarnation of Mrs. Smith's Roger—one Roger-Isarn de Fanjeaux, who died in prison in 1243. In her incarnation as his lover, Mrs. Smith had gone to the stake with the other martyred Cathars.

Eventually, Guirdham assembled a circle of eight people who seemed to remember lives as Cathars. Their community was beset by apparently paranormal happenings. Spectral Cathar spirit entities were said to have visited them, and on the anniversary of the Cathar holocaust, several of the group suffered severe physical pain. It is said one woman even exhibited stigmata in the form of fiery blisters.

Criticized as unscientific and uncooperative in helping independent researchers verify his story, Guirdham nevertheless maintained that he and the others had undergone several reincarnations as a group. He wrote three books on the case, which remains among the most intriguing in reincarnation lore.

A member of Guirdham's circle allegedly made this drawing when she was seven years old. It is said to depict two Inquisitors killed by the Cathars, as well as an English child's attempt to render "Avignonet"—a site where Cathars were massacred—in her own language.

new life it assumes a new physical form: human, animal, or even vegetable. That form, whether higher or lower than the preceding one, is determined by the karma or ethical conduct followed in the previous life. The law of karma presumes that there is an inevitable punishment or reward which follows every act, thought, attitude, and aspiration and that the atman thus generates its own favorable or unfavorable destiny in the next life.

Acts of hostility or acts that in any way harm other creatures are believed to have a particularly negative effect on karma, as does passive ignorance that leads to such destructive behavior. By the same token, acts of mental and physical self-discipline, such as the system of exercises known as yoga, can contribute positive karma; through them the atman can eliminate human error and sensuality. When the atman finally develops all the capacities latent in human nature, and thus reaches complete spiritual insight, its journey ends in a final transcendent union with the world spirit.

This new metaphysic was shared in its basic outlines by most of the major formal religions that arose in ancient India—by Brahminism, or Hinduism, which embraced it virtually whole, and by Buddhism and Jainism, which came along somewhat later and recast the idea of rebirth in slightly different forms. Buddhists, for example, reject the idea of the soul that persists unchanged from one life to the next. Rather, they believe that when people die they are survived by a dynamic complex of personality and character traits and memories that are always changing, much as genetic material passes on from generation to generation in a continuous flow, each time expressed differently. A person may be reborn into any of five classes of living beings: gods, human beings, animals, hungry ghosts, or the damned. Buddhists hold that rebirth ends when the three "fires"—craving, ill-will, and ignorance—are ultimately extinguished, a condition and place signified in the word Nirvana.

Modern American and European interest in reincarnation began to grow in the mid-nineteenth century, at about the same time that spiritualism came into vogue. Indeed, the word reincarnation itself was introduced in the 1860s by Allan Kardec, a leading French believer who, in his *The Spirits' Book,* laid out a lengthy argument for rebirth, which he saw as a matter of choice rather than necessity. According to Kardec, spirits dissatisfied with their current level of spiritual growth could

opt to return for another chance, as could those seeking revenge for some wrong. Living persons, he wrote, might become aware of a past life either through spontaneous memory or through dreams.

The launching of the Society for Psychical Research in England in 1882 gave reincarnation another small boost,

A 1985 mass cremation in a Balinese village features huge wooden effigies that hold coffins containing the remains of children who died during the previous twenty-two years. Cremations are joyous occasions in Bali, where the religion is mostly a mixture of Hinduism and a local animism. Followers believe cremation frees the soul for reincarnation. Thus some families keep the remains of their dead for years, waiting to accumulate enough funds for a proper funeral.

signifying as it did the willingness of the intellectual establishment to acknowledge the possibility of paranormal phenomena. The notion of rebirth was also given considerable currency by the Herculean work of Madame Helena Blavatsky, whose Theosophical Society borrowed from Eastern religions the concepts of karma and reincarnation. Among the westerners attracted to her teachings were such prominent figures as the inventor Thomas A. Edison and poets Alfred Lord Tennyson and William Butler Yeats.

Nevertheless, the notion of reincarnation is still rejected by most scientists and academics in the West, although the meticulous attention it has received from serious students like Ian Stevenson in the United States and his counterparts in Europe and Asia has earned it some measure of grudging toleration. And public opinion polls have shown that a sizable minority of westerners believe in some aspects of reincarnation—when they were questioned in 1969, 20 percent of the Americans, 25 percent of the West Germans, 23 percent of the French, and 18 percent of the British reported that they accepted the notion; when Americans were polled again in 1981, the figure had climbed three more points.

Researchers who probe the possibilities of reincarnation generally divide the evidence into three categories. The first embraces spontaneous episodes, in which people—most frequently children—seem to have vivid memories of what they believe to be a prior life, apparently without any sort of external prompting. The second type of evidence comes from hypnotic regression, a practice that has only recently achieved some small measure of respectability. The final category of reincarnation cases, and the weakest in the opinion of most researchers, involves third parties who purport to serve as channels of communication between a past personality and a living person.

Investigators who delve into cases of spontaneously recalled lives have accumulated the thickest dossier of reincarnation evidence—although the quality of the evidence varies widely. Dreams are regarded as one pathway for spontaneous reincarnation messages. Indeed, in cultures that readily accept reincarnation, pregnant women often report dreams in which a dead person comes to them with the information that his or her spirit will be reborn in the body of their child. Scenes from supposed earlier lives may also appear in dreams. For example, a British woman once told of a recurrent dream in which she and a playmate fell from a high gallery to a floor of black and white marble squares in an old rectory. On visiting a supposedly haunted house, she said, she recognized it as the setting of her dream, and learned that centuries earlier a young brother and sister had fallen to their deaths on the marble floor. When she saw a pair of miniature portraits displayed in the house, she immediately identified them as "my mother and father." It turned out that the two were in fact the parents of the children who had fallen to their deaths long ago.

Traumatic accidents are another pathway to spontaneous recall. The remarkable case of Dorothy Eady—alias Bentreshyt, alias Omm Sety—is one such example. Dorothy Eady's odyssey began in London in 1907 when, according to her reminiscences, she fell down a flight of stairs at the age of three. A physician pronounced her dead of her injuries, but minutes later she was found to be alive. From the time of the accident onward, she insisted that England was not her real home and that she felt estranged from everything around her. As she grew older and became acquainted through magazines and the British Museum with ancient Egypt, she became convinced that Egypt was where she belonged.

In dreams, Dorothy Eady came to know herself as Bentreshyt, a young Egyptian girl of the nineteenth dynasty, some 3,200 years ago. By her account her parents, unable to care for her, had left her at the Temple of Sety at Abydos, south of Thebes, when she was three. Taken into the temple as a sacred virgin, she became a priestess of Isis and eventually caught the eye of King Sety I. They became lovers in secret because their liaison was a violation of religious law; Bentreshyt, finding herself pregnant, committed suicide to cover up the crime.

Meanwhile, Dorothy Eady was encouraged by her father, a cinema operator and small-time showman, to perform on the stage of his movie house. Often her act had an exotic twist, as when she sang "Somewhere in the Sahara" or the "Lament of Isis and Nephthys." But all this was pro-

American statesman and scientist Benjamin Franklin may have believed in reincarnation. Reincarnationists contend he had rebirth in mind when, as a young printer, he wrote a whimsical epitaph promising to come back "In a New and more Elegant Edition, Revised and Corrected By the Author."

logue to the real business of her life, which began when, at the age of twenty-nine, she met an Egyptian man who was studying in London. Joining him after he returned to Cairo, she became his wife and bore a child, whom she named Sety. Legally an Egyptian citizen now, Dorothy divorced her husband; eventually she would take for herself the name of Omm Sety, or "mother of Sety."

Thanks to demonstrated knowledge of her favorite subject, Dorothy won a job as a draftsman and editor with the Egyptian Department of Antiquities. She also resumed an active involvement with her past life. As she told the story, the ancient King Sety became in her present life her lover once again, both spiritually and physically, through a form of astral projection. She also claimed to make periodic visits to the Egyptian afterworld, where she met the pharaoh Ramses II along with other important figures from history.

Native Egyptians were not quite certain what to make of her, nor was the self-styled Omm Sety herself absolutely sure about how to assess her stories. Once, she cheerfully conceded that there were those who maintained that she had "knocked a screw loose" during her childhood fall down the stairs. Whatever the sources of her past-life recollections, when she died in her beloved city of Abydos in 1981 she was a popular if eccentric figure. Her last wish, however, was left unfulfilled. In the years before her death, she had painstakingly prepared a decorative underground tomb, complete with a figure of Isis, in the garden behind her modest home. But the local health authorities refused to permit her to be buried there; her remains were interred instead in the desert northwest of the Temple of Sety.

Another frequently cited example of allegedly spontaneous past-life memories involves a set of British twin girls *(pages 110-111).* Born to John and Florence Pollock on October 4, 1958, Jennifer and Gillian were believed by their father and mother to be the reincarnated spirits of older daughters Joanna and Jacqueline, who had been killed by an automobile while walking to church one Sunday morning in 1957. What made the case particularly unusual is the fact that both parents were Roman Catholics, ordinarily not the sort of people to give credence to reincarnation. But John, a convert to Catholicism at the age of nineteen, had always held a personal, if slightly clandestine, belief in reincarnation—so much so that he repeatedly prayed to God for some proof. When Joanna and Jacqueline died, he feared that their loss was intended as some kind of punishment for

his heresy, but when he learned soon after that he was about to become a father again, he saw the event as God's favorable answer to his prayers. He told his wife that she would bear not one child, as the doctor assured her, but two, and that they would be girls.

After the twins' births, their father noted many curious similarities between them and their deceased older sisters: a scarlike mark on Jennifer's forehead that seemed to match one on Jacqueline's forehead, instances in which the twins claimed to recognize landmarks of which they could not reasonably have had any knowledge, a shared fear of a car under circumstances matching that of their sisters' death. But researchers like Ian Wilson, the British author of *All in the Mind,* a skeptical book about reincarnation, hold the opinion that the simplest explanation is probably the best— that the twins were sensitized to their father's feelings and convictions from a very early age and that they thereby unconsciously gathered all sorts of messages from him. As

Two more American pragmatists who believed in reincarnation were inventor Thomas Edison (right) and industrialist Henry Ford, who may have discussed it on one of their many camping trips in the 1920s.

such, his wishes literally became father to their deeds.

Visions of supposed previous lives sometimes appear to be triggered by visits to sites that were frequented by a person during some earlier incarnation. For example, George S. Patton, the great American general of World War II, never doubted what he called the "subconscious memories" in which he saw himself as a warrior who had fought and died in battle many times throughout history: He believed, for example, that he had served as a soldier under Alexander the Great, with the Roman legions, and with Napoleon, among others. Of course, Patton's visions may have been traceable to nothing more than a wide knowledge of military history and a self-dramatizing imagination, but he himself sometimes appeared to be surprised by them. His first such experience occurred when he was a young officer in France during World War I *(pages 12-13)*. Another took place in 1943, after Patton had defeated the Axis forces in Sicily. Given a tour of the island, the general repeatedly interrupted his astonished guide by pointing out the sites and details of obscure historical events. Finally, the guide asked him if he had been there before. "I suppose so," Patton replied, though this was in fact his first visit to Sicily.

Patton's seeming remembrances of scenes from the past were in a way similar to the almost universal experience of déjà vu, the momentary sensation of witnessing a scene or an event we have seen before but have no clear recollection of and cannot explain. Researchers believe that most déjà vu incidents are either genuine memories that we have forgotten or recollections of things that have been learned secondhand but have become tangled or confused in our minds as personal experiences. Other déjà vu sensations can be explained physiologically: The brain sometimes produces what amounts to a double exposure, two glimpses—a fraction of a second apart—of a remembered scene, which the mind mistakenly takes to be widely separated in time; blinking at the right moment can have a similar effect.

Serious reincarnation investigators take a dim view of most déjà vu cases. But some reports, if true, seem to indicate something beyond forgotten memories or physiological quirks. One such story tells of a British youth who was touring caves formerly used as prisons on the isle of Guernsey when he claimed to remember watching, in a former life, a prisoner being sealed in a cavern at the site. Officials denied any such incident, but when the boy persisted, they launched a search; behind a bricked-up entrance they found a skeleton. According to the boy's mother, who reported the incident to a reincarnation researcher nearly twenty-five years after her son's death in 1935, a search of the old prison's archives revealed an inmate with the same name as the one given by her son for the walled-in prisoner.

Equally intriguing is the case of a young woman who told her story to the paranormal researcher D. Scott Rogo. In the 1970s, she claimed, she was driving on the New Jersey Turnpike when she suddenly had the eerie feeling that everything she was seeing was familiar, even though she knew for a fact that she had never been there before. She told her driving companion that "about a mile or so down the road is a house I used to live in," and went on to predict what other sights lay ahead. She then exited from the highway and approached a small town, which she described in advance; there she saw the very porch where, perhaps eighty years earlier, she had sat with her grandmother. Rogo's informant went on to claim that she then described a certain drugstore, with a high marble counter, where her grandmother would take her for lemonade. "The building was still there, much the same as it used to look, but it was boarded up, and we could not look inside . . . .I 'knew' that I had died when I was about six or seven years old." She wanted to try to find her grave, which she said was in a cemetery just over the hill, but her friend, too frightened to continue, insisted on getting back in the car and leaving.

As suggestive as such reports may be, reincarnation researcher Ian Stevenson maintains that the most useful spontaneous recall cases come from young children. They are less likely than others to have absorbed information from written or other sources that might then be consciously or unconsciously reproduced as a past-life story. Indeed,

Omm Sety (below), who believed she was the reincarnation of an Egyptian priestess beloved of Pharaoh Sety I, poses in Abydos in 1958 at the Osirion, said to have housed part of the dismembered body of the god Osiris. At left, Sety I, in bas-relief on a wall in the Temple of Sety at Abydos, offers a golden collar to Osiris.

Although from childhood she considered Egypt home, Omm Sety began life—her most recent one, at least—as a middle-class English girl named Dorothy Eady. One of the few photographs from her pre-Egyptian days shows her in 1920 amid the blooms of her native country. On the back of the picture she wrote: "Sweet 16 & still a virgin."

youngsters often begin talking about prior lives before they are old enough to read. Stevenson also finds useful the fact that preschool-age children tell their stories without interpretation and in a take-it-or-leave-it style. The cases are also easier to verify because the previous lives that were recalled by children often came to an end within the memory of people still living.

In gathering all the verification he can, Stevenson tries to eliminate in systematic fashion every alternative explanation for a child's recollections, including fraud, unconscious memories, and even such paranormal phenomena as extrasensory perception (ESP) and possession. (ESP is understood to mean the reception of information through sources other than the five senses; in cases of alleged possession, subjects appear literally to become the people they were, whereas people claiming reincarnation merely remember that they have lived before but are not now the individuals they were then.)

To be sure, the ideal case that would furnish irrefutable proof of reincarnation still eludes Stevenson. That case would have to meet his own rather rigorous requirements: first, numerous and unusual details about the earlier life that prove accurate under close examination; second, a written record of the child's claims made before a serious investigator becomes involved, so as to avoid contamination by design or by inadvertent leading questions; third, behavioral similarities between the present and past personalities—a habit, a tic, a way of laughing, for example; fourth, a current birthmark corresponding to a mark or wound that appeared on the past-life person's body; and fifth, in the instance of the past-life person's having spoken a different dialect or language from that of the current incarnation, knowledge of that dialect or language during spontaneous memory.

While searching for the elusive perfect case, Stevenson has noted several recurrent patterns among the allegedly reborn toddlers he has studied. Most, for example, begin to speak of their prior lives between the ages of two and four years—as soon as they can talk coherently—and they normally stop between about five and eight. (The Sri Lankan boy Sujith stopped talking about Sammy sometime after his sixth birthday.) In cases that have been studied closely, roughly 90 percent of the verifiable "memories" turn out to be accurate. In most cases the child lives within a few miles of the past-life predecessor and speaks the same language. And, perhaps least surprising, the frequency of cases is particularly high in countries such as India and Burma, where reincarnation is an article of faith.

There also tends to be a pattern within cultures regarding the "intermission," or time between lives, and the prevalence of reincarnation within generations of the same family. Tibetan Buddhists, for example, believe that the usual intermission is a mere forty-nine days between one life and the next. Sex changes seem to occur with frequency from one life to the next among cultures that believe them possible, such as the Burmese and the Kutchin Indians of northwestern Canada, but not among those that do not, such as the Syrian Druse and the Tlingit Indians of Alaska.

Whether they come from the East or the West, a preponderance of supposedly reborn children recall having died violently. The number of violent deaths thus reported consistently exceeds the mortality rates normal for the subjects' countries, and the children's memories often center on the events just preceding their past-life demise. Stevenson speculates that the shocking intensity of such deaths might specifically "enhance and preserve memories" in a way that death from failing health might not. Indeed, the children he studies often suffer from phobias connected with the cause of their previous-life death. As Sujith was afraid of trucks, other children who claim to have been murdered or drowned in previous lives exhibit fears of knives or water.

Birthmarks corresponding to marks on a past-life body or deadly wounds suffered in that life seem strikingly common, too. Stevenson's records showed more than 250 birthmark cases as of 1983. He found that 51 percent of the Tlingit Indians of Alaska who professed rebirth had such corresponding birthmarks. One elderly Tlingit predicted just before his death that his spirit would be reborn in his niece's still unborn child and that she would recognize the truth of what he said in the two marks on the baby's body that would match those on the old man, including a surgical scar on his back. Indeed, the woman's child was born with those precise markings, the back scar bordered by tiny round marks that Stevenson described as "lined up like stitch wounds" from surgery.

The story of an Indian boy named Ravi Shankar (no relation to his gifted countryman, the sitar player, of the same name) illustrates many of the recurrent elements in Stevenson's findings and also contains an additional ingredient that brings it closer than most to the perfect case—a birthmark. In 1953, when Ravi was two, he started talking about a former life in a neighboring district. He described several of his previous-life toys—a wooden elephant, a ball on an elastic string, a toy pistol—as well as a ring he kept in a desk. He mentioned the name of his previous father, who he said was a barber. Ravi then shocked everyone by insisting that he had been murdered. He identified his murderers by name and occupation, recalled that he had been eating guavas just before he was killed, and said that his slayers had cut his throat.

When Ravi was four, a man who had heard about the stories visited the family and told them that his own six-year-old son had been killed six months before Ravi's birth in the exact way Ravi had described. The names and occupations of the men identified by Ravi matched those of two men related to the victim, who were believed to have committed the murder to secure an inheritance. The bereaved father went on to say that one of the alleged murderers had confessed but later recanted the confession and was freed for lack of evidence.

Stevenson set out to investigate the incident in 1964, by which time Ravi was thirteen. He discovered that a teacher had taken notes on Ravi's claims when he was five, and Stevenson was able to confirm twenty-six statements of fact the boy had made, among them the specific toys, the

ring in the desk, and the guavas the victim had eaten before he was attacked. Stevenson learned that the two families had a "nodding acquaintance" but that Ravi's father had tried to silence his son, beating him severely on occasion to make him stop talking about his previous life. The investigator thus thought it unlikely that Ravi had been told about the murder by his parents. As a child, Ravi had a phobia about knives and razors and was afraid to go to the area where the other boy had been killed. And then there was the eerie scar on his neck, which his mother had first noticed when he was three months old. When Stevenson saw it, the birthmark was two inches long and a quarter-inch wide, though he was told it had been longer before. Darker than the surrounding skin, the mark had "the stippled quality of a scar," he wrote. "It looked much like an old scar of a healed knife wound."

In another Indian case that Stevenson investigated, the details were even more bizarre, because they seemed to suggest that reincarnation had taken place in a living child who had come close to dying but survived—or seemed to survive. The parents of three-year-old Jasbir Lal Jat thought their son had died of smallpox; his breathing had stopped and his body had turned cold. But the next day the child stirred, and within a few weeks he recovered completely.

His behavior changed dramatically, however. He now claimed that he came from a town about twenty miles away and belonged to a higher, Brahmin caste. The boy refused to eat the food his mother cooked on the grounds that it was not made in the Brahmin manner, and he spoke in a more sophisticated way as befitted his claimed estate. He said that his earlier life had precipitously ended when he fell from a chariot in a wedding procession. His disastrous fall, he said, was the result of his having eaten some poisoned sweets, given to him by a man to whom he had lent money. The poison had made him giddy, causing him to lose his balance and suffer a fatal head injury.

Jasbir's family were troubled by the boy's strange behavior, and except for making arrangements with a kindly

Brahmin neighbor to prepare his food, they tried to suppress evidence of the goings on in their house. But word of his claims did leak out to other Brahmins in the community and eventually to the village where he said he had lived before. Relatives of the late Sobha Ram Tyagi heard the story and, because Sobha Ram had died in a chariot accident about the time that Jasbir had suffered his brush with death, they were eager to question the boy. When they visited Jasbir's home, he greeted them by name and later ticked off several facts about their life. Subsequently, Jasbir visited the Tyagis's village, repeatedly demonstrated a familiarity with places and people there, and was reluctant to return home to his own family.

Stevenson later talked to both families and corroborated thirty-eight statements made by Jasbir about Sobha Ram's life. He confirmed that, in the opinion of everyone who knew the child, Jasbir became noticeably different—a different person, one might say—after his recovery (and coincident with Sobha Ram's death). Reincarnation was, in Stevenson's view, one possible explanation, although a case might also be made for spirit possession.

Stevenson's critics, while acknowledging his high standards and often compelling collections of evidential details, fault his conclusions on several grounds. Ian Wilson contends that some evidence in both the Sujith and the Ravi Shankar cases, for example, indicates that the supposedly reborn children or their families may have learned more about their earlier "lives" from other people than they let on. He also suggests that some poor Indian families may claim higher-caste previous lives for their children in the hope of acquiring for themselves either financial or psychological advantage in this life.

Wilson, D. Scott Rogo, and Professor C. T. K. Chari, an Indian parapsychologist, all argue that Stevenson is so committed to reincarnation as an explanation for his suggestive evidence that he gives short shrift to other paranormal possibilities or alternatives. One such notion cited by Wilson is the possibility that mothers may somehow transmit their own traumatic memories, visions, or dreams to the unborn children in their wombs. Fetuses are known to be sensitive to a variety of stimuli originating outside the womb, and Wilson wishes that Stevenson had, at the very

Joanna Pollock was eleven years old and her sister Jacqueline six when a car struck and killed them on this quiet English street in Hexham, Northumberland, in 1957. The following year, Gillian and Jennifer Pollock (inset) were born. Their father firmly believed the twins were reincarnations of the daughters he had lost. John Pollock averred that as toddlers the girls remembered living previously as their older sisters, recognized their belongings and surroundings, and resembled them in certain physical marks. A simpler explanation might be that the father, wittingly or otherwise, imbued the twins with his own strong faith in reincarnation.

least, included in his research questions to the mothers about their experiences before and during pregnancy.

Stevenson's defenders, among them psychologist Alan Gauld of the University of Nottingham and James G. Matlock, librarian and archivist at the American Society for Psychical Research, reply that Stevenson himself, in his scrupulous case studies and cautious arguments, provides most of his critics' ammunition. And they point out that he meticulously examines all sides of every case before reaching the careful, low-key conclusion that reincarnation is at least possible if not proven.

While Stevenson sifts through his mounds of evidence for reincarnation, other investigators probe the alleged past-life memories of their subjects through hypnotic regression. Stevenson, for one, takes a dim view of most testimony gathered by this means, but the hypnotic technique is practiced widely and is well-covered by popular writers in the field. To conduct a session of hypnotic regression, a practitioner needs no props but his or her own rhythmic, droning voice to induce a trancelike state in which the subject's concentration is increased at the same time that peripheral awareness, or distractibility, is reduced. No extraordinary powers are required to induce hypnosis; the willing cooperation and trust of the patient are usually enough. The accepted wisdom is that about 10 percent of the population is immune to hypnosis, 80 percent can be put into a light trance, and the other 10 percent—the elite among hypnotic subjects—enter a deep trance. Among the trance-talented, remarkable effects can follow: surgical patients, for example, can forgo anesthesia, and hemophiliacs can substantially reduce their bleeding tendencies.

For purposes of reincarnation study, a hypnotist typically uses suggestion to regress subjects back to childhood and then induce them to leap the void to a time before their present lives. Often enough the images thus triggered are intense and detailed, although most subjects cannot remember subsequently what they said while in a trance.

Quite apart from seeking evidence of past-life experi-

ences, some psychiatrists and psychologists also use hypnotic regression as a therapeutic technique for dealing with disabling fears. In the controversial practice known as "past-life therapy," the hypnotist guides a patient through a reliving of a traumatic experience in a previous life that purportedly explains a phobia or other symptom in this one *(pages 88-95)*. One practitioner, California psychologist Helen Wambach, claims that past-life therapy cured a woman suffering from dizzy spells by leading her back to an incarnation in which she was pushed off a cliff.

One problem with hypnotic regression in reincarnation research is that it is extremely difficult, if not impossible, to screen out the subject's conscious or unconscious adoption of clues that are suggested by the hypnotist. Studies have shown that hypnotic subjects are often eager to give a hypnotist whatever they think he or she wants to hear and that their stories become more elaborate as their sessions progress. Stevenson maintains that suggestibility is at the root of most past-life regressions and compares the resultant tales to dreams. "Nearly all hypnotically evoked 'previous personalities' are entirely imaginary," he declares, "just as are the contents of most dreams."

A second problem falls in the general category of abnormal memory—often termed cryptomnesia—a phenomenon that can reveal itself when the subject is undergoing hypnotic regression. In cases of cryptomnesia, subjects tap into a detailed memory of something of which, when they are in a normal state of consciousness, they are unaware. Although it may appear to be information gathered in an earlier life, and thus evidence of reincarnation, the possibility that subjects are calling up from their subconscious mind material that was gathered in a long-forgotten book, movie, or television show cannot be ruled out easily.

A classic example of cryptomnesia was recounted by a Canadian psychologist, who described putting one of his patients under hypnotic regression, only to have him begin to write at length in a strange language. When the patient came out of his trance, he was unable to recognize what he

had written or explain its origin. The doctor, fascinated by this curious occurrence, sought the help of linguists, who eventually identified the writing as Oscan, a precursor of classic Latin. The patient swore he knew nothing of the language, but after extensive questioning, the doctor was able to trace the source to an occasion many years earlier when his subject had spent an afternoon in a library, sitting next to someone engaged in research. That individual, it turned out, had his book open to a page on which an ancient Oscan curse was recorded. The doctor's patient had merely glanced over at his neighbor's work, but in the process had taken a mental snapshot of the open page. The image of the esoteric writing registered so strongly on his unconscious memory that it remained there ready to be called up again when the right circumstances—the heightened concentration of the trance state—presented themselves.

Another favorite example of cryptomnesia is the story

of one Countess Maud, allegedly a fourteenth-century Englishwoman, who played a starring role in the persuasively detailed recollections of a hypnotic subject in England in 1906. The portrait of Maud was exquisitely rounded; it included what she ate, how she dressed, her friends—a veritable treasure of medieval trivia that turned out to be correct in almost every particular. And with good reason: As a sleuth for the British Society for Psychical Research proved, the historical details were all from a little-known story the subject eventually remembered having read. Its title was "Countess Maud."

Acknowledging the potential for contamination by suggestion and cryptomnesia, the more scrupulous hypnotic regressionists look for alternative explanations for their subjects' stories before accepting them as evidence of reincarnation. At the same time, the colorful stories that unreel under hypnosis are the most exciting and dramatic in the literature of reincarnation. And they can exert an extraordinary power over those relating them, regardless of the source or the validity of the outpourings. For example, when a British newspaper in 1956 conducted a contest to elicit proof of reincarnation, hypnotist Henry Blythe stepped forward to demonstrate the past-life existence of one Mary Cohen in a vigorous thirty-two-year-old subject named Mrs. Naomi Henry. With reporters looking on, Blythe asked the supposed Mary Cohen to recall her life at a series of ages. Her voice and manner seemed to grow progressively older as she proceeded. When Blythe asked her finally to describe herself at seventy, she failed to respond to two consecutive questions. He realized to his horror that she was no longer breathing, that her pulse had stopped, and that the color had drained from her face. The frightened hypnotist told

Mrs. Henry that she was safe, and she resumed breathing. On further questioning, she revealed that the putative Mary Cohen had died at the age of sixty-six. Chastened by this apparent brush with death, the newspaper that had been conducting the contest called off all further experiments.

One of the most compelling and best-documented examples of hypnotic regression is the story of Graham Huxtable, a soft-spoken swimming instructor from Swansea, South Wales. At about the same time that Henry Blythe was conducting his experiments with Naomi Henry, Huxtable agreed to become a past-life regression subject with a Welsh hypnotist named Arnall Bloxham. Bloxham put Huxtable under hypnosis and, as he did with his hundreds of other patients, carefully tape-recorded the proceedings.

Soon after Huxtable entered the trance state, he seemed to become one Ben, a master gunner on an eighteenth-century British frigate he called *Aggie.* At the outset Huxtable/Ben responded, albeit impatiently, to the interviewer's questions, but as the session went on Ben took over entirely, ignoring his interrogator and becoming wholly engrossed in his role. Clearly tense with anticipation, he prepared his invisible gun crew to battle an approaching French vessel. His voice grew loud and raucous, and his speech heavily accented and full of obscure eighteenth-century nautical terminology.

From Ben's disjointed comments, Bloxham was able to piece together the following dramatic scenario. H.M.S. *Aggie* was commanded by a Captain Pearce ("He's fond of the cat," Ben said, referring to the cat-o'-nine-tails, the favorite device for keeping insubordinate sailors in line. "Aye, too fond.") The vessel was lying off Calais, waiting for "the bloody Frogs, aye, Frenchies . . . ah, God, wish they'd come," Ben said. Minutes later, the French are sighted, and the gunner begins speaking with growing urgency and excitement as he cautions his men: "Steady, lads, steady. Now hold it, hold it, hold it, wait for the order. Swing those matches [tar-soaked rope lengths that were lit and used to fire the guns]." When the order comes, Ben bellows "NOW, YOU FOOL! NOW UP, FOOL, NOW. NOW!" And as the shots are fired he screams in exultation.

Ben continues to order his men about, praising, scolding, and cheering them on as they reload their guns and fire repeatedly. "WELL DONE LADS, RUN 'EM UP! GET 'EM UP!" Then, seemingly in the heat of pitched battle, he shrieks: "Pull that man out, pull 'im out!" There is another apparent salvo, and Ben shouts: "Hurry men! By God you bastard! Got him that time. That's the way to lay a gun. My Christ, they've got old Pearce, they've got Pearce!" At that, Ben pauses for a moment, then screams out: "MY BLOODY LEG! MY LEG! MY LEG!"

Bloxham had trouble bringing Huxtable back from the trance state, and when the subject finally emerged he complained of a pain in his leg. As Huxtable listened to the tape he professed astonishment at what he heard come out of his mouth. The swimming instructor had never been to sea, he said, nor was he particularly interested in naval history. Experts later verified the slang and dialect Ben used, but they could find neither a ship named (or nicknamed) *Aggie* nor a Captain Pearce in the naval records of the time. (Critics note that it is often the case in hypnotic regression that peripheral details, such as archaic speech, curious customs, and odd sights, can be verified as appropriate to the time and place, but central facts, such as the actual existence of a named person or place, prove elusive, thus leaving the entire story unproven.)

On the other hand, no book or film that might have implanted such a story in Huxtable's unconscious could be traced either. Surely, Ben's tale brimmed with authenticity and conveyed a potent sense of reality. If Huxtable was not actually reliving a past life, say some researchers, he was certainly drawing on powers of recall or invention that are equally mysterious.

Intriguing and tantalizing as such stories may be, the all-time superstar among past-life subjects remains Virginia Tighe. The wife of a Pueblo, Colorado, businessman, she proclaimed while under hypnosis that she had lived in Ireland more than a century earlier as one Bridget (Bridey)

Reincarnation or Recall?

It may be that many so-called past-life memories are attributable to cryptomnesia, not reincarnation. British hypnotherapist Joe Keeton has regressed more than 9,000 people and believes that hidden memory figures in most instances—but not all.

One exceptional case he cites is that of Ray Bryant, who, under hypnosis, seemed to remember being an infantry sergeant in the Crimean War. According to Keeton, Bryant's descriptions of battles contained accurate details unavailable from history books. His stories paralleled accounts in letters written by a young officer to his mother during the conflict—letters donated by the family to a museum but never published.

Whatever the source of Bryant's memories, some details apparently were erroneous. When his regression was chronicled on the television program "Beyond Explanation," he mentioned using a Hammond rifle in the Crimea. Melvin Harris, the program's researcher, points out the Hammond was not used there. The rifle that was actually used required new methods of loading that a soldier would scarcely forget. Moreover, Bryant said he remembered that during the Battle of the Alma, there was smoke from a burning wagon. In fact, smoke blanketed the battlefield because the Russians had burned a neighboring village.

Like many others of its kind, this case remains intriguing but unresolved.

A death certificate shows that Reuben John Stafford, supposedly the soldier of Ray Bryant's past life, drowned in 1879. He was an apparent suicide.

In what some see as a pilgrimage to his own grave, Bryant visits the London cemetery where Stafford is buried.

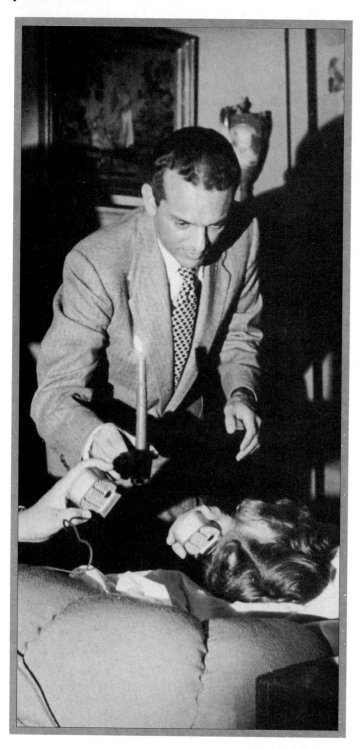

Murphy. And the name of Bridey Murphy would be forever enshrined in the public mind as the quintessential example of a previous life revealed by hypnotic regression.

The Tighe/Murphy story was first brought to light by Morey Bernstein, an experienced hypnotist living in Pueblo. Bernstein in effect discovered the mysterious Irishwoman, and detailed his conversations with her in a 1956 book titled *The Search for Bridey Murphy*. His story, which was first serialized in newspapers in 1954, became an international sensation, propelling the subject of reincarnation onto front pages over the world.

Bernstein called Tighe by the pseudonym of Ruth Simmons to preserve her privacy, for she feared that her in-laws would look askance at a respectable Christian woman who dabbled in hypnosis and reincarnation. At the time of the hypnosis sessions, she was a twenty-nine-year-old mother of three. Born in Madison, Wisconsin, and a resident of Chicago for several of her formative years, she would later claim never to have visited Ireland or to have had any special association with Irish people. (Bernstein also insisted that he had no personal knowledge of Ireland.) Yet, she was able to give a wonderfully detailed account of Bridey's life in nineteenth-century Ireland.

Bridey appeared after Bernstein had first regressed Mrs. Tighe to childhood and then encouraged her to "go to some other place in some other time" (critics later accused him of leading her). "Scratched the paint off all my bed . . ." were her first words, referring to an incident in her alleged earlier childhood. Speaking in an Irish brogue, she said that she grew up in the city of Cork in a Protestant family that consisted of her father, Duncan, a barrister, her mother, Kathleen, and a brother also named Duncan. Constantly probing for verifiable details, Bernstein elicited a birth date in 1798 and a description of her death sixty-six years later, after breaking a hip. Bridey "just sort of withered away," she said, and after her funeral, at which a man played the "uilleann pipes," she was "ditched," or buried.

Specifics of all kinds—names, dates, places, events,

customs, songs, shops—tumbled out of her as Bernstein's tape recorder rolled through six separate sessions. Bridey said she was married in a Protestant ceremony at the age of twenty to Sean Brian Joseph McCarthy, a Catholic and son of a Cork barrister. Brian, as she called him, had also studied law, and after they were wed they moved to Belfast, where he taught at Queen's University. To satisfy Brian's family, they were married a second time in a Catholic service at Belfast's Saint Theresa's Church, by Father John Joseph Gorman. On another occasion she described the cliffs of Antrim that she had seen as a child ("the streams run down real fast and make little rivulets in the ground"), the stores where she shopped in Belfast (Farr's for food, John Carrigan's greengrocery), and her favorite meal (potato cakes, which she called by their colloquial name, "platters"). At one point she said she could dance the "morning jig," and under a posthypnotic suggestion from Bernstein, Virginia Tighe performed a lively little dance.

Much of the appeal of Bridey's story lay in just such ordinary detail, the accumulation of commonplace facts and incidents. And when Tighe returned to consciousness after each session, she was invariably surprised. She could not account for the source of any of the information played back to her on tape.

When Bernstein probed further and asked Bridey about the interval between one life and the next, she mentioned "a place of waiting . . . where everybody waits," a realm without day or night or death or disease or families. There, she told him, she could travel by merely willing herself to be somewhere else. In time she learned of her imminent rebirth from "some women," and then she simply

The unassuming Virginia Tighe shrank from her Bridey Murphy notoriety. "All I know," she said, "is that as far as I am concerned, the story is completely honest."

"passed to another existence."

Bridey's story proved so intriguing, and touched such a receptive chord in people's imagination, that it was published in thirty countries and serialized in dozens of newspapers. Bartenders concocted Bridey Murphy cocktails, disc jockeys played "The Ballad of Bridey Murphy," comedians told reincarnation jokes ("I've changed my will—I'm leaving everything to myself," quipped one), and in California a self-described "Mr. Hypnosis" offered clients a tour of their prior lives at twenty-five dollars per life. "Come as you were" parties enjoyed a brief vogue, too. On a darker note, however, a Shawnee, Oklahoma, youth shot himself to death because, as he said in the suicide note he left: "They say that curiosity kills a cat. I'm a cat and I'm very curious about this Bridey Murphy story so I'm going to investigate the theory in person."

Meanwhile, journalists pawed through dusty Irish records in an effort to confirm or contradict the numerous details in Bridey's tale. The results of their search were mixed. Many of her statements proved to be correct, or at least they were consistent with the earlier time and place. Among these were her description of the Antrim cliffs, her identification of merchants Farr and Carrigan, and the uilleann pipes that she said were played at her funeral. Bridey also seemed to know things that could only have been learned in Ireland, and with difficulty even there.

Those eager to debunk her story took comfort from the reporters' failure to find any specific traces of Bridey or her family. Indeed, no records corroborated her account of her birth, marriage, or death, but that could just as well have been because the government's vital statistics records did not go back that far; only a family Bible was likely to

The ruins of Dunluce Castle on the shore of County Antrim, Ireland, were correctly described by Tighe.

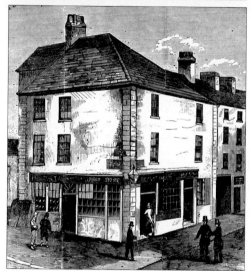

Tighe was not always right. The wooden houses she placed in Antrim are, in fact, made of stone.

contain the kinds of data wanted, and finding that in a country with literally tens of thousands of Murphys was a task too great even for the swarms of self-appointed investigators crawling over the Irish countryside.

On the other hand, some of Bridey's memories were found on examination to be just plain wrong, and her language was not always reliable either. Sometimes spiced with Irish vernacular ("linen" for handkerchief), her speech also contained glaring examples of twentieth-century American speech ("downtown," for example). A Chicago newspaper, which looked into Virginia Tighe's early years in that city, claimed that the source of Bridey's information was actually an Irish-born woman that Tighe had known as a child, but this exposé all but evaporated on investigation. The woman in question was never shown to have spent time in Virginia's company, much less to have regaled her with Irish dialect stories, and the fact that she was the mother of one of the very editors involved in writing the debunking articles in the first place would seem to cast even further doubt on the newspaper's objectivity.

The final judgment on Bridey Murphy is yet to be delivered. Mrs. Tighe rejected nightclub offers and other opportunities to capitalize on her transitory celebrity. Bernstein's earnest openness and what *Life* magazine called his awed "what-have-I-wrought style" helped his credibility. The best reporter on Bridey's trail, William Barker of the *Denver Post,* came away persuaded that her story had "the ring of truth, whatever that truth ultimately means." Ian Wilson, surely no advocate of reincarnation, saw "evidence for something as yet unexplained" in Bridey's saga. And Ian

Stevenson counts the Bridey Murphy phenomenon as a rare exception to his general dismissal of hypnotic regression cases. Virginia Tighe's remembrance of her life as Bridey could still turn out to be a subconscious fantasy rooted in an unfound book or a forgotten childhood experience, but Stevenson does not think so. He believes her memories were "somehow acquired paranormally."

While most reincarnation researchers seek evidence in the testimony of those who appear to have recollections of their alleged past lives, others have pointed to the performance of child prodigies, whose skills appear so early in life that some observers have contended that they must be holdovers from an earlier existence. Some notable examples include Wolfgang Amadeus Mozart, who composed mature music at five; an eighteenth-century French boy named Jean Cardiac, who reportedly knew the alphabet when he was three months old and could speak a half-dozen languages at the age of six; and a sightless four-year-old slave child called "Blind Tom" in pre-Civil War Georgia, who was able to play the piano the first time he sat down at a keyboard. A teacher who came to examine this last child declared that "he knows more of music than we know or can learn." Psychologists, however, maintain that child prodigies such as these are merely born with mental quirks that give them highly retentive memories and a superior ability to organize their thoughts.

A far more compelling category of reincarnation research is the study of a phenomenon parapsychologists call xenoglossy, or the speaking of foreign languages. This occurs when people who are apparently reliving an earlier in-

Critics said the real Bridey Murphy was Bridie Corkell of Chicago, shown here with her grandchildren. Out to undercut the Chicago Daily News's syndication of Bernstein's book, the rival Chicago American reported that as a child, Tighe lived near Corkell, knew her well, and modeled the "reincarnation" on her. But this story had many flaws and was little less suspect than the reincarnation itself.

carnation seem able to speak a language they do not know in their present life. To Ian Stevenson's way of thinking, "responsive xenoglossy," in which the speaker is able to converse spontaneously with another (as distinct from speaking in a self-directed monologue), is a skill that cannot be transmitted either normally or paranormally from one person to another; it must be learned the hard way, through practice. One of the few reasonably well-documented examples thus far uncovered is that of T.E./

Jensen Jacoby, which was investigated at length by Stevenson beginning in 1958.

T.E., whose full identity has never been revealed because of her desire for privacy, was a thirty-seven-year-old Philadelphia housewife at the time of the experiments. The hypnotist was K.E., her husband, who was both a physician and a sometime experimenter in hypnotic regression. When K.E. led T.E. into the trance state, which he did on at least eight different occasions, she seemed to become a farmer named Jensen Jacoby (who claimed to have lived three centuries before), with a voice suddenly transformed from the female range to one that was distinctly deep and masculine. In the first few sessions, "Jacoby" spoke in broken English, but his speech gradually became more and more infused with Swedish words. By the sixth session the subject was conversing exclusively in Swedish with several Swedish-speaking persons who had been invited to listen in. Sometimes Jacoby's responses were, by Stevenson's judgment, "sluggish" and repetitive, resembling those of "a person with an organic brain syndrome such as delirium or in a state of complete exhaustion." At other times farmer Jensen Jacoby's expression became animated and emotional, as when talking about his intense dislike for war and fighting. Once, he treated his audience to a reportedly spirited rendition of a drunk on a binge.

No one could produce a rational explanation for T.E.'s newfound language ability. Her parents were Russian immigrants, but they rarely spoke any language save English at home, and when they or their relatives did resort to another language, it was invariably Polish or Russian, tongues linguistically quite distant from Swedish. K.E. also disclaimed any knowledge of Swedish. Nor had T.E. ever studied that Scandinavian language or associated with Swedes. The only Swedish connection Stevenson found was a popular television series on Swedish immigrants in America, which T.E. had watched. Yet, in one session T.E./Jacoby was shown several artifacts from a Swedish museum, including a model of a seventeenth-century ship, and was able to identify most of them by their correct Swedish names. The native

Lives of the Dalai Lama

In 1950, the Chinese began overrunning Tibet, looting and razing thousands of the inland nation's Buddhist temples and monasteries. The invaders thus destroyed the outward signs, at least, of an ancient religion whose faithful had for some 500 years looked for temporal and spiritual leadership to a single figure, a man-god known as the Dalai Lama.

The Dalai Lama's significance rests with age-old Tibetan Buddhist tenets regarding reincarnation. Like Hindus, Buddhists believe that souls transmigrate. The blessed fate for those enlightened souls that have expunged all karma is Nirvana, a blending with transcendental universal unity and cessation of the endless round of death and rebirth. However, the advanced soul may choose to postpone Nirvana and remain on the wheel of reincarnation in order to help other souls toward enlightenment. Such a being is called a bodhisattva, a Sanskrit word meaning awakening warrior. Bodhisattvas vow not to enter Nirvana until all other souls have preceded them.

Among these semidivine beings, none is considered to be more sacred by Tibetan Buddhists than Avalokitesvara, the Bodhisattva of Compassion. And each Dalai Lama is believed to be an incarnation of Avalokitesvara—a single soul, heir to the wisdom of many lifetimes.

After the death of the first Dalai Lama in 1475, monks set out to find his successor in a child believed to have been chosen by Avalokitesvara for his next incarnation. This practice of succession through reincarnation persisted through the centuries to the current Dalai Lama, the fourteenth, who fled from his Tibetan palace to exile in India in 1959.

This gilt copper figure is a depiction of the Bodhisattva Avalokitesvara, whose soul is held to inhabit every Dalai Lama.

Oracular signs direct the search for each new Dalai Lama. There may be dreams or visions to indicate his general whereabouts, his age, or his physical characteristics. When the child is found, he is tested to determine the authenticity of his incarnation. The primary requirement is that from an array of objects he be able to identify those belonging to his predecessor. Correct choices are crucial, since Tibetan Buddhists believe that those who choose rebirth retain the memory of their past lives.

Although he ranks highest among them, the Dalai Lama is but one of many Tibetan Buddhist leaders whose continuous succession relies on reincarnation. The high Panchen Lama, for example, is believed to be the manifestation of Amitabha, Bodhisattva of Unlimited Light and the father of Avalokitesvara.

In fact, any lama—a term encompassing Buddhist monks and priests, as well as nuns and even very holy laypeople—may be reincarnated in the body of a child. Such reincarnations, including those of high lamas, are called *tulku*. Tulku may be of either sex, although the Dalai Lama has always been male.

All tulku are said to be conscious of their previous existences. Thus, in earlier days it was not uncommon in Tibet for a child to inform his parents of past-life status as an abbot, perhaps, or as a venerated elder. If the parents believed the claim, they might have sought an investigation by lamas who could affirm or disprove it. Reincarnations of holy laypeople had scant practical importance. But tulku believed to be reincarnated religious leaders were invested with all the property and prerogatives belonging to their predecessors.

The current Dalai Lama (left), born in 1935, was a toddler living on his family's farm when searchers disguised as pilgrims found him. He wrote later that he penetrated their disguise at once and ran to greet the strangers as old friends. Rearing against the Tibetan sky, the thirteen-story Potala Palace (below) is traditionally the sacred residence of the Dalai Lama. "Potala" means "the holy abode of Avalokitesvara."

Swedish speakers who were present at the session testified that Jacoby's Swedish was archaic and laced with some Norwegian but seemed generally correct for its time, and that the subject handled the most difficult to pronounce words with ease. Jacoby also answered a long list of questions in Swedish and volunteered dozens of Swedish words. Still not satisfied, however, Stevenson had T.E. take the Modern Language Aptitude Test to see if she had some unrecognized ability for languages. She scored poorly.

This degree of skill in a second language, Stevenson concluded, ruled out cryptomnesia, telepathy, and extrasensory perception. He also investigated the possibility of fraud on the parts of either T.E. or K.E., and after lengthy interviews with others who knew the couple, as well as a

Only ten months after his birth in Lübeck in 1721, Christian Heinrich Heinecken could talk. By age two he purportedly had mastered biblical history. By three he could speak French and Latin, plus his native German, and was soon versed in geography and ancient and contemporary history. He died at four, already a legend as "The Infant of Lübeck."

Some believe child prodigies demonstrate wisdom accumulated from past lives. Wolfgang Amadeus Mozart, shown performing with his father, Leopold, and his sister, Maria, began composing at four. He wrote his first symphony at eight, his first opera at twelve.

battery of personality tests, lie detector tests, and consideration of possible motives for so elaborate a deception, the doctor finally determined to his satisfaction that everyone was telling the truth. In his opinion, all that remained as possible explanations for T.E.'s xenoglossy were reincarnation and possession.

Critics, including Wilson and Rogo, have never been convinced, however. T.E.'s continuing anonymity, they point out, has made independent verification by others impossible. More troubling, they say, is the fact that subsequent to the Jensen Jacoby episodes, T.E. became a trance medium on her own, suggesting that she had more than a passing interest in paranormal phenomena. Furthermore, she was found on two occasions to have notes in her possession that were identical in wording to the oral "messages" she delivered in a trance. But none of these problems would seem to discount her ability to answer unrehearsed questions in an alien language. Like Bridey Murphy, Jensen Jacoby can still be classed as a still-unsolved puzzle.

Most of those who speak in trances of past lives purport to be divulging details of their own previous existences. In some cases, however, trance mediums and other psychic practitioners claim the ability to report on the earlier incarnations of others. One of the best-known such figures was Edgar Cayce,

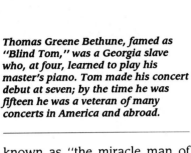

Thomas Greene Bethune, famed as "Blind Tom," was a Georgia slave who, at four, learned to play his master's piano. Tom made his concert debut at seven; by the time he was fifteen he was a veteran of many concerts in America and abroad.

known as "the miracle man of Virginia Beach" and "the sleeping prophet"—the latter for his practice of making pronouncements while in a sleeplike stupor.

The mild-mannered Cayce began life in Kentucky in 1877, the son of a farmer with a strong attachment to fundamentalist Christianity. Uneducated beyond the seventh grade, he was a sometime Sunday school teacher and insurance salesman-photographer when he suddenly lost his voice. Put into a hypnotic trance, he diagnosed and apparently cured his own ailment. In full voice again, he set out to learn what other wonders he could work while in the trance state.

He soon discovered that he had a gift for healing others, and he began a remarkable new career as a medical diagnostician, prescribing cures for physical ailments while entranced. Sometimes he performed his "examination" in person, sometimes across hundreds of miles with nothing but the unseen patient's vital statistics to go by.

French scientist and philosopher Blaise Pascal was a prodigy in mathematics. By sixteen he had discovered what he called his "mystic hexagram," proposing the theorem on which projective geometry came to be based.

Cayce would put himself into a trance, picture his "patient," and come up with medical advice that, if followed faithfully, reportedly produced genuine recoveries in many cases. Later, as his fame grew, the sleeping prophet branched out from the treatment of physical ills and began giving so-called life readings, in which he told of people's previous lives to help them better cope with the present.

Cayce identified the source of his knowledge as "the Akashic records," said to be a sort of cosmic register of all phenomena throughout history. His own past, he said, included lives as a high priest in ancient Egypt, an early Christian, and a British soldier in prerevolutionary America. When giving a reading (and he gave some 2,500 during his career), Cayce put himself into a trance, after which the relevant information (name, birthdate, and a few personal details) about the person consulting him was read aloud by an assistant. With eyes closed the seer then gave his response.

Often, he told of previous lives in the legendary lost land of Atlantis, though former Atlanteans were generally said to have had numerous intermediary existences before arriving in modern times. In one case, for example, Cayce told how a fourteen-year-old Alabama boy had served earlier as a wardrobe master to King Louis XIV—the Sun King—of France; a tradesman in classical Greece; an ancient Egyptian priest; and, earliest of all, an Atlantean prince who went by the name of Amiaie-Oulieb, whose untimely death by drowning had kept him from ascending a royal throne. Another young boy's previous lives were traced through North America during the French and Indian War, Western Europe at the time of the Huns and Goths, ancient Egypt, and then on to Atlantis, where he had allegedly been among the libertines whose excesses of the flesh had led to the island continent's downfall and destruction.

Like the Hindus and Buddhists, Cayce attached great signficance to the karma principle; evils in a past life must be paid for by mortal suffering in this one, and only recognition of one's past transgressions and a certain amount of atonement could bring relief. Cayce's life readings tended to divide all problems into one of three kinds of karma, popularly described as boomerang karma, organismic karma, and symbolic karma. Typical of boomerang karma was the blind college professor, whom Cayce found to have been in a past life a Persian marauder in the habit of blinding victims with a red-hot poker. The organismic karma of a past-life glutton might turn up in this life as a digestive disorder. And symbolic karma could take any number of subtle forms, from deafness in the person who turned a deaf ear to the sufferings of others in a past life to shortness of stature in one who may have been haughty.

Cayce's followers, who preserve the archives of thousands of diagnoses and life readings at their Virginia Beach, Virginia, headquarters, say that some past-life identities have been historically verified. But other investigators, Ian Stevenson among them, maintain that such verification of these alleged former incarnations is spotty at best. "In the vast majority of cases," he has noted, "it has not been possible to trace the existence of the person mentioned or identified as having been in a previous existence the person for whom the reading was given."

In recent years, the best-known exponent of reincarnation revelations by trance mediums has probably been the actress Shirley MacLaine, an avid believer in numerous paranormal phenomena. The irrepressible MacLaine believes that in one earlier life she was a Mongolian teenager, in another she was Louis XV's court jester, and in a third a prostitute—"it's no accident I played all those hookers" in the movies, she has said. MacLaine, who has written several books recounting her spiritual odyssey, claims to be in touch with "an astonishing and moving world of psychic phenomena where past lives, the existence of spirit guides, and the genuine immortality of the soul . . . [are] more than

concepts to me." She accepts karma as "a simple cosmic law that what you put out, you get back. One tries in each life to transcend prior failures."

The pursuit of an explanation that ties up every loose end in the vast literature of reincarnation has intensified in recent years, but it is still far from over. Indeed, the search may turn out to be a quest that has no end, an expedition into the unknowable where certainty will always be an elusive stranger. Dedicated researchers, of course, do not allow such possibilities to deter them from trying, and so they go on comparing, theorizing, analyzing, and finally, yearning for definitive proof or disproof.

A formidable number of scientific-minded investigators lean to cryptomnesia as at least a partial explanation for the origins of most reincarnation tales. Thanks to the unraveling of the celebrated Countess Maud story, and to the sleuthing that finally solved the mystery of the Toronto man with the uncanny knowledge of ancient Oscan, we do know that the mind is able to store and absorb phenomenal amounts of material, putting it into a kind of personal Akashic record. There remains, of course, the question of why different individuals store different kinds of arcane data. One explanation is that the mind selectively gathers the data that it transforms into "memories" on the basis of present-life traumas. In one case, for example, American psychologist Edwin Zolik showed that a man's story of a past-life career as a lonely nineteenth-century riverman derived from a movie he had seen coupled with his own buried feelings of isolation from his parents.

Finnish psychiatrist Reima Kampman shares this view. Kampman, who has conducted years of research into the origins of past-life experiences, is convinced that past-life regressions are explainable as an expression of "hypnotically-induced multiple personality." He has found in a large sample of volunteer students that 7 percent were able to produce past lives under hypnosis and that among the segment capable of going into deep trance, the percentage of self-styled past-lifers swelled to forty-one. But most of these subjects, when questioned thoroughly under hypnosis, were able to give Kampman enough clues to the origins of these second selves that the psychiatrist could trace their stories to rather mundane contemporary sources. Kampman also demonstrated that the students who recalled past lives most readily were emotionally healthier and better adjusted than those who resisted the hypnotic experience. He reasons that the egos of this receptive group are secure enough to be able to tolerate the kind of mind adventure that might be threatening to people who are less sure of themselves.

Ian Stevenson also credits cryptomnesia as "probably the principal explanation . . . which must be excluded" before any paranormal hypotheses are considered. He also rejects genetic or inherited memory—the idea developed by the pioneering Swiss psychiatrist Carl Jung that we are born with certain racial or familial memories, in the same

Finnish psychiatrist Reima Kampman's research makes a strong case for cryptomnesia as the source of past-life memories. Under hypnosis, some of his subjects have even recalled page numbers in books that were sources for buried memories mistaken for earlier incarnations.

way we are born with certain human instincts. To Stevenson's way of thinking, too many purported rebirths cross family and even cultural borders for that explanation to hold up. In addition, he doubts that ESP is responsible, because few of the subjects have seemed to manifest any such gift, and because it fails to explain the presence of a skill like xenoglossy or the complex patterns of behavior that usually accompany past-life experiences. Possession, too, can be ruled out, according to Stevenson, for past-life memories are too fragmentary; a person who is "possessed" by someone else would presumably know more about that other life than most subjects seem to.

And so the tantalizing mystery of reincarnation seems for the moment to remain open. For the many individuals who steadfastly accept the proposition that the physical act of dying means utter extinction, that nature's iron laws leave no room for the survival of a spirit of any kind, the argument is at best irrelevant. Others, moved by curiosity or hope, may eagerly welcome what Ian Stevenson, judicious as always, has called "a growing body of evidence that permits a rational belief in reincarnation, even though this evidence falls far short of being decisive."

A Wheel of Life and Death

To live is to suffer. To die is to be born again and suffer. The cycle of life and death and reincarnation, known as Samsara, wheels endlessly, inexorably. Release comes only through Enlightenment, the compassionate awareness of the universal oneness of all things. Enlightenment is the door to Nirvana, an escape from the wheel, a merging with the oneness.

These are tenets of Buddhism, which also holds that suffering comes from the ego's self-awareness, its illusion of a distinction between self and other. The Buddha taught that no deity will aid the quest to shed such shackling illusion. Individuals determine their own fate, creating with deeds and thoughts the karmic ledger governing progress toward Enlightenment. The journey may be incalculable, requiring many successive lives in human and other forms, in this and other worlds.

Elegant in its simplicity, Buddhism has assumed complexity in its 2,500-year history and its spread from India to other lands. The religion often blended peacefully with preexisting faiths. In Tibet, for example, it incorporated aspects of an animistic religion called Bon. Thus Tibetan Buddhism has come to include intricate rituals and ceremonies and a panoply of heavens and hells, gods and demons. Unperturbed by such paradoxical infusions, Buddhists note serenely that whatever the path to Enlightenment, the goal is unchanging and inevitable.

In this Tibetan painting, Yama, Lord of Death, grips the Wheel of Becoming, which depicts the cycle of death and rebirth. At its center are a pig, a rooster, and a serpent, symbolizing ignorance, desire, and aggression, respectively.

A lama, or monk, performs a New Year ceremony to banish
the demon of unmanageable ego. Mystical power to repel evil spirits
supposedly invests each detail of his elaborate costume.

A reminder of the body's impermanence, a human skull trimmed in
silver (right), holds ritual wine, which is used in initiation
ceremonies for monks. This vessel is from the Potala Palace in Lhasa.

Prayer flags called lung ta, "horses of the wind," beseech present happiness and future Enlightenment. Winds that touch them are said to bless all they touch thereafter.

A nun, her head shaved, holds prayer beads in her left hand and a prayer wheel in her right. Peculiarly Tibetan, the wheel is rotated in reenactment of Buddha's turning the Wheel of Law, setting in motion Buddhist doctrine.

Monks meditate beneath richly embroidered hangings in the Drepung Monastery's Rtsho-chen Hall. The enormous fifteenth-century monastery is northwest of the town of Lhasa.

A painting on cloth of the meditating Buddha on a lotus seat is a typical tanka, religious art used by Buddhists to aid their meditation. This painting, by a Tibetan Buddhist monk, comes from Katmandu, Nepal.

Ominous-looking bird-headed gods, messengers of higher deities, are common figures in Tibetan art. Buddhists expect to meet them in the netherworld, should fate require a temporary sojourn there.

A lama reads to old people from the Tibetan Book of the Dead, teaching what awaits them in the Bardo, a shadowy realm between death and rebirth. Unlike Western cultures, which fearfully avoid the subject, Buddhism teaches that death is but a natural progression of the soul. Dying is an art, fully equal to the art of living. To die well and bravely, to die transcending bodily pain and holding right thoughts, is to help assure a propitious rebirth. Thus, dying earns intensive study, especially among the elderly

In a ritual called the Celestial Burial, a lama feeds a dismembered corpse to vultures. Repellent to some westerners, fo

etan Buddhists this ceremony is a soul-freeing affirmation and a final act of charity, celebrating reverence for all life

ACKNOWLEDGMENTS

The index was prepared by Hazel Blumberg-McKee. The editors wish to thank these individuals and institutions for their valuable assistance in the preparation of this volume: Dr. Susan Blackmore, Bristol, England; Ray Briant, Reading, England; Chief Librarian, National Library of Ireland, Dublin; Mr. and Mrs. John Clark, Florence, Italy; Nicholas Clarke-Lowes, Society for Psychical Research, London; Hugh Downs, Jr., Berkeley, Calif.; Foreign Languages Press, Beijing, China; Dr. Keith Harary, Institute for Advanced Psychology, San Francisco; Melvin Harris, Benfleet, Essex, England; Dr. Reima Kampman, PsychoSoma Oy Tampere Suomen Kuvapalvelu Oy, Helsinki; Joe Keeton, Hoylake, Lancashire, England; Don Ferdinando and Donna Maresti Massimo, Rome; Deng Ming, Deputy Editor-in-Chief, Shanghai People's Art Publishing House, Shanghai; Nancy Moneagle, Monroe Institute of Applied Science, Faber, Va.; Braham Norwick, New York; Eleanor O'Keefe, Society for Psychical Research, London; Dr. Garrett Oppenheim, Tappan, N.Y.; Oratorian Fathers, S. Maria in Vallicella (Chiesa Nuova), Rome; Tamara Saslow, Yonkers, N.Y.; Shanghai People's Art Publishing House, Shanghai; Nicholas P. Spanos, Carleton University, Ottawa, Canada; Fabian Tassano, Institute of Psychophysical Research, Oxford; Jeanette Thomas, Association for Research and Enlightenment, Virginia Beach, Va.; Mrs. James W. Totten, South Hamilton, Mass.; Ian Wilson, Bristol, England; Shen Xifei, Vice Director, Foreign Languages Press, Beijing, China.

BIBLIOGRAPHY

Abbott, Eugenie B., "The Miraculous Case of Blind Tom." *The Étude Music Magazine* (Philadelphia), August 1940.

Alain, Pierre, *The Great Places of France.* Transl. by Evelyn Rossiter. Fribourg, Switzerland: Productions Lieber SA, 1982.

Aldridge, Alfred Owen, *Benjamin Franklin and Nature's God.* Durham, N.C.: Duke University Press, 1967.

Ayer, Fred, Jr., *Before the Colors Fade: Portrait of a Soldier, George S. Patton, Jr.* Boston: Houghton Mifflin, 1964.

Baker, Carlos, *Ernest Hemingway: A Life Story.* New York: Avon Books, 1968.

Banerjee, H. N., *Americans Who Have Been Reincarnated.* New York: Macmillan, 1980.

Bassuk, Daniel E., *Incarnation in Hinduism and Christianity.* Atlantic Highlands, N.J.: Humanities Press International, 1987.

Bernstein, Morey, *The Search for Bridey Murphy.* Garden City, N.Y.: Doubleday, 1956.

Blackmore, Susan J.:

Beyond the Body. London: William Heinemann, 1982.

"Out-of-the-Body Experiences." In *Psychical Research,* ed. by Ivor Grattan-Guinness. Wellingborough, Northamptonshire, England: Aquarian Press, 1982.

Bleiler, E. F., "The Mummy Made Her Do It" (book review of *The Search for Omm Sety* by Jonathan Cott). *Washington Post,* July 5, 1987.

Blumenson, Martin:

The Patton Papers: 1885-1940. Boston: Houghton Mifflin, 1972.

Patton: The Man behind the Legend, 1885-1945. New York: William Morrow, 1985.

Blythe, Henry, *The Three Lives of Naomi Henry.* New York: Citadel Press, 1956.

Bowles, Norma, Fran Hynds, and Joan Maxwell, *Psi Search.* New York: Harper & Row, 1978.

Bradbury, Will, ed., *Into the Unknown.* Pleasantville, N.Y.: Reader's Digest, 1981.

Bradley, David G., *A Guide to the World's Religions.* Englewood Cliffs, N.J.: Prentice-Hall, 1963.

Brean, Herbert, "Bridey Murphy Puts Nation in a Hypontizzy." *Life,* March 19, 1956.

"Bridie Search Ends at Last." *Life,* June 25, 1956.

Brier, Bob, *Ancient Egyptian Magic.* New York: Quill, 1981.

Bryan, Michael, *Bryan's Dictionary of Painters and Engravers.* Ed. by George C. Williamson. Port Washington, N.Y.: Kennikat Press, 1964.

Buckley, Peter, *Ernest.* New York: Dial Press, 1978.

Butlin, Martin, *Paintings and Drawings of William Blake.* Vols. 1 and 2. New Haven, Conn.: Yale University Press, 1981.

Calloway, Hugh G. (pseud. Oliver Fox), *Astral Projection: A Record of Out-of-the-Body Experiences.* New Hyde Park, N.Y.: University Books, 1962.

Casson, Lionel, and the Editors of Time-Life Books, *Ancient Egypt* (Great Ages of Man series). New York: Time-Life Books, 1965.

Cavendish, Richard, ed.:

Encyclopedia of the Unexplained. New York: McGraw-Hill, 1974.

Man, Myth & Magic. New York: Marshall Cavendish, 1985.

Cerminara, Gina, *Many Mansions.* New York: William Sloane, 1950.

Cerri, Oreste, *S. Filippo Neri—Aneddotico.* Rome: Edizione Il Villaggio del Fanciullo di Vergiate, 1986.

Christie-Murray, David:

"The Language of the Dead." *The Unexplained* (London), Vol. 1, Issue 7.

"Memories, Dreams or Inventions." *The Unexplained* (London), Vol. 1, Issue 9.

"Other Voices, Other Lives." *The Unexplained* (London), Vol. 1, Issue 3.

Reincarnation. London: David and Charles, 1981.

Christopher, Milbourne, *Search for the Soul.* New York: Thomas Y. Crowell, 1979.

Clifford, Terry, "Shirley MacLaine's Spiritual Dance." *American Health,* January-February 1987.

Connery, Donald S., *The Inner Source.* New York: Holt, Reinhart and Winston, 1982.

Cook, Emily Williams, "Research on Reincarnation-Type Cases." In *Case Studies in Parapsychology,* ed. by K. Ramakrishna Rao. Jefferson, N.C.: McFarland, 1986.

Cott, Jonathan, "Walk Like an Egyptian." *Omni,* July 1987.

Cott, Jonathan, with Hanny El Zeini, *The Search for Omm Sety: A Story of Eternal Love.* Garden City, N.Y.: Doubleday, 1987.

Cranston, Sylvia, and Carey Williams, *Reincarnation: A New Horizon in Science, Religion, and Society.* New York: Julian Press, 1984.

Crookall, Robert:

Case-book of Astral Projection. Secaucus, N.J.: University Books, 1972.

Out-of-the-Body Experiences: A Fourth Analysis. Secaucus, N.J.: Citadel Press, 1970.

The Study and Practice of Astral Projection. Secaucus, N.J.: Citadel Press, 1960.

Curley, Michael J., *Physiologus.* Austin: University of Texas Press, 1979.

(His Holiness the) Dalai Lama of Tibet, *My Land and My People.* New York: McGraw-Hill, 1962.

Davenport, Marcia, *Mozart.* New York: Charles Scribner's Sons, 1960.

Dawson, Jenny, "The Disembodied Self." *The Unexplained* (London), Vol. 1, Issue 6.

Deford, Frank, "Shirley MacLaine." *People,* July 18, 1983.

Dickinson, G. Lowes, "A Case of Emergence of a Latent Memory under Hypnosis." *Proceedings of the Society for Psychical Research* (Glasgow, Scotland), August 1911.

Douglas, Alfred, *Extra-sensory Powers.* Woodstock, N.Y.: Overlook Press, 1976.

Ducasse, C. J.:

"Bridey Murphy Revisited." In *Reincarnation in the Twentieth Century,* ed. by Martin Ebon. New York: World, 1969.

"The Doctrine of Reincarnation in the History of Thought." *International Journal of Parapsychology* (New York), summer 1960.

Durant, Will, *The Story of Civilization:*

Part 1, *Our Oriental Heritage.* New York: Simon and Schuster, 1954.

Part 2, *The Life of Greece.* New York: Simon and Schuster, 1966.

Part 3, *Caesar and Christ.* New York: Simon and Schuster, 1944.

Eastman, Margaret, "Out-of-the-Body Experiences." *Proceedings of the Society for Psychical Research* (London), Vol. 53, 1960-1962.

Ellison, A. J.:

"Fact, Imagination or Psi?" *The Unexplained* (London), Vol. 6, Issue 72.

"Points of View." *The Unexplained* (London), Vol. 6, Issue 71.

Evans-Wentz, W. Y., comp. and ed., *The Tibetan Book of the Dead.* London: Oxford University Press, 1960.

"Eye to (Third) Eye." *Science News,* November 9, 1985.

Fairley, John, and Simon Welfare, *Arthur C Clarke's World of Strange Powers.* New York: G. P. Putnam's Sons, 1984.

Farago, Ladislas, *Patton: Ordeal and Triumph.* New York: Dell, 1963.

Ford, Paul Leicester, *The Many-Sided Franklin.* New York: Century, 1899.

Fox, Oliver, *Astral Projection.* New Hyde Park, N.Y.: University Books, 1962.

Gabbard, Glen O., and Stuart W. Twemlow, *With the Eyes of the Mind.* New York: Praeger, 1984.

Gallup, George, Jr., with William Proctor, *Adventures in Im-*

mortality. New York: McGraw-Hill, 1982.

Garraty, John A., and Peter Gay, eds., *The Columbia History of the World.* New York: Harper & Row, 1972.

Garrison, Webb B., "Blind Tom: Mystery of Music." *Coronet,* July 1952.

Gauld, Alan:

The Founders of Psychical Research. London: Routledge & Kegan Paul, 1968.

Mediumship and Survival. London: William Heinemann, 1982.

Gilchrist, Alexander, *Life of William Blake.* New York: E. P. Dutton, 1942.

Gill, Brendan, *Lindbergh Alone.* San Diego: Harcourt Brace Jovanovich, 1971.

Grattan-Guinness, Ivor, ed., *Psychical Research.* Wellingborough, Northamptonshire, England: Aquarian Press, 1982.

Great Religions of the World. Washington, D.C.: National Geographic Society, 1971.

Green, C. E., *Lucid Dreams.* Oxford, England: Institute of Psychophysical Research, 1968.

Greyson, Bruce, and Charles P. Flynn, eds., *The Near-Death Experience: Problems, Prospects, Perspectives.* Springfield, Ill.: Charles C Thomas, 1984.

Grosso, Michael, "Recollections of Death: A Medical Perspective" (book review). *Anabiosis* (Storrs, Conn.), December 1981.

Grosvenor, Donna K., and Gilbert M. Grosvenor, "Bali by the Back Roads." *National Geographic,* November 1969.

Guirdham, Arthur:

The Cathars & Reincarnation. London: Neville Spearman, 1970.

We Are One Another. London: Neville Spearman, 1974.

Guru Rinpoche, *The Tibetan Book of the Dead.* Transl. by Francesca Fremantle and Chögyam Trungpa. Berkeley, Calif.: Shambhala, 1975.

Hall, Alice J., "Philosopher of Dissent: Benj. Franklin." *National Geographic,* July 1975.

Hall, Angus, *Strange Cults.* Garden City, N.Y.: Doubleday, 1976.

Hall, Manly P., *Spiritual Centers in Man.* Los Angeles: Philosophical Research Society, 1978.

Head, Joseph, and S. L. Cranston, comps. and eds.:

Reincarnation. New York: Causeway Books, 1967.

Reincarnation: The Phoenix Fire Mystery. New York: Julian Press, 1977.

Hemingway, Ernest, *A Farewell to Arms.* New York: Charles Scribner's Sons, 1929.

Hobbs, A. Hoyt, and Joy Adzigian, *A Complete Guide to Egypt and the Archaeological Sites.* New York: William Morrow, 1981.

Hogan, Robert, *Dictionary of Irish Literature.* Westport, Conn.: Greenwood Press, 1979.

Holms, A. Campbell, *The Facts of Psychic Science and Philosophy.* New Hyde Park, N.Y.: University Books, 1969.

Holroyd, Stuart:

Minds without Boundaries. London: Aldus Books, 1976.

Psychic Voyages. Danbury, Conn.: Danbury Press, 1976.

The Horizon History of Christianity, by the Editors of *Horizon Magazine.* New York: American Heritage, 1964.

Hövelmann, Gerd H., "Evidence for Survival from Near-Death Experiences? A Critical Appraisal." In *A Skeptic's Handbook of Parapsychology,* ed. by Paul Kurtz. Buffalo: Prometheus Books, 1985.

Hutchens, John K., "Roundup to Date on Bridey Murphy." *New York Herald Tribune,* March 11, 1956.

"In Her Own Words." *People,* April 30, 1984.

Iverson, Jeffrey, *More Lives Than One?* New York: Warner Books, 1976.

Jicheng, Li, and Ku Shoukang, *The Realm of Tibetan Buddhism.* San Francisco: China Books & Periodicals, 1985.

Jigmei, Ngapo Ngawang, et al., *Tibet.* New York: McGraw-Hill, 1981.

Kampman, Reima, *Hypnotically Induced Multiple Personality.* Oulu, Finland: University of Oulu, 1973.

Kastenbaum, Robert J., *Death, Society, and Human Experience.* Columbus, Ohio: Charles E. Merrill, 1986.

King, Francis, "Blavatsky: Larger Than Life." *The Unexplained* (London), Vol. 9, Issue 104.

Kinkead, Eugene, "Have You Lived Before?" (interview with Ian Stevenson). *Family Circle,* June 14, 1978.

Kline, Milton V., ed., *A Scientific Report on the Search for Bridey Murphy.* New York: Julian Press, 1956.

Kübler-Ross, Elisabeth:

On Death and Dying. New York: Macmillan, 1969.

To Live until We Say Goodbye. Englewood Cliffs, N.J.: Prentice-Hall, 1978.

Kupferberg, Herbert, *Amadeus: A Mozart Mosaic.* New York: McGraw-Hill, 1986.

LaBerge, Stephen, *Lucid Dreaming.* Los Angeles: Jeremy P. Tarcher, 1985.

Lacey, Robert, *Ford: The Men and the Machine.* Boston: Little, Brown, 1986.

Langley, Noel, *Edgar Cayce on Reincarnation.* New York: Warner Books, 1967.

Larsen, Caroline D., *My Travels in the Spirit World.* Burlington, Vt.: Lane Press, 1927.

"Leaving the Body," In *Into the Unknown,* ed. by Will Bradbury. Pleasantville, N.Y.: Reader's Digest, 1981.

Levine, Art, Cynthia Kyle, and Peter Dworkin, "Mystics on Main Street." *U.S. News & World Report,* February 9, 1987.

Levy, G. R., ed., *The Myths of Plato.* Carbondale, Ill.: Southern Illinois University Press, 1960.

Lindbergh, Charles A.:

Autobiography of Values. New York: Harcourt Brace Jovanovich, 1978.

The Spirit of St. Louis. New York: Charles Scribner's Sons, 1953.

Lundahl, Craig R., comp., *A Collection of Near-Death Research Readings.* Chicago: Nelson-Hall, 1982.

MacLaine, Shirley:

Dancing in the Light. New York: Bantam Books, 1985.

Out on a Limb. New York: Bantam Books, 1983.

Madaule, Jacques, *The Albigensian Crusade.* Transl. by Barbara Wall. London: Burns & Oates, 1967.

Magré, Maurice, *Magicians, Seers, and Mystics.* Transl. by Reginald Merton. New York: E. P. Dutton, 1932.

Martin, Anthony, *The Theory and Practice of Astral Projection.* Wellingborough, Northamptonshire, England: Aquarian Press, 1980.

Monroe, Robert A., *Journeys Out of the Body.* Garden City, N.Y.: Doubleday, 1971.

Moody, Raymond A., Jr.:

Life after Life. Harrisburg, Penn.: Stackpole Books, 1975.

Reflections on Life after Life. Harrisburg, Penn.: Stackpole Books, 1977.

Moore, R. Laurence, *In Search of White Crows.* New York: Oxford University Press, 1977.

Muldoon, Sylvan, and Hereward Carrington:

The Phenomena of Astral Projection. Albuquerque, N.Mex.: Sun Books, 1981.

The Projection of the Astral Body. York Beach, Maine: Samuel Weiser, 1986.

Mullin, Glenn H., *Death and Dying: The Tibetan Tradition.* Boston: Routledge & Kegan Paul, 1986.

"Near-Death Experiences Illuminate Dying Itself." *New York Times,* October 28, 1986.

Netherton, Morris, *Past Lives Therapy.* New York: William Morrow, 1978.

New Catholic Encyclopedia. New York: McGraw-Hill, 1967.

Noyes, Russell, Jr., "Dying and Mystical Consciousness." *Journal of Thanatology,* January-February 1971.

Noyes, Russell, Jr., and Roy Kletti, "The Experience of Dying from Falls." *Omega,* February 1972.

Oppenheim, Garrett, "Who Were You before You Were You?" *Venture Inward* (Virginia Beach, Va.), May-June 1987.

Osis, Karlis, and Erlendur Haraldsson, *At the Hour of Death.* New York: Avon Books, 1986.

Osis, Karlis, and Donna McCormick, "Kinetic Effects at the Ostensible Location of an Out-of-Body Projection during Perceptual Testing." *Journal of the American Society for Psychical Research,* July 1980.

Parton, James, *Life and Times of Benjamin Franklin.* New York: Da Capo Press, 1971.

Perry, Michael, "Psychical Research and Religion." In *Psychical Research,* ed. by Ivor Grattan-Guinness, Wellingborough, Northamptonshire, England: Aquarian Press, 1982.

Picknett, Lynn, "At Death's Door." *The Unexplained* (London), Vol. 6, Issue 62.

Plato, *The Dialogues of Plato.* Transl. by Benjamin Jowett. Chicago: William Benton, 1952.

Probst, George E., ed., *The Indispensable Man.* New York: Shorewood, 1962.

Province, Charles M., *The Unknown Patton.* New York: Hippocrene Books, 1983.

Reston, James, Jr., "Mission to a Mind." *Omni,* July 1984.

Richardson, H. E., *A Short History of Tibet.* New York: E. P. Dutton, 1962.

Ring, Kenneth:

Heading toward Omega. New York: William Morrow, 1984.

Life at Death: A Scientific Investigation of the Near-Death Experience. New York: Quill, 1980.

"Precognitive and Prophetic Visions in Near-Death Experiences." *Anabiosis* (Storrs, Conn.), June 1982.

Ritchie, George G., with Elizabeth Sherrill, *Return from Tomorrow.* Old Tappan, N.J.: Spire Books, 1978.

Rogo, D. Scott:

Leaving the Body. New York: Prentice-Hall, 1983.

Life after Death. Wellingborough, Northamptonshire, England: Aquarian Press, 1986.

"Researching the Out-of-Body Experience." In *Case Studies in Parapsychology,* ed. by K. Ramakrishna Rao. Jefferson, N.C.: McFarland, 1986.

The Search for Yesterday. Englewood Cliffs, N.J.: Prentice-Hall, 1985.

Ross, Nancy Wilson, *Buddism: A Way of Life and Thought.* New York: Vintage Books, 1980.

Sabom, Michael B., *Recollections of Death: A Medical Investigation.* New York: Harper & Row, 1982.

Sety, Omm, and Hanny El Zeini, *Abydos: Holy City of Ancient Egypt.* Los Angeles: L L Company, 1981.

Sheils, Dean, "A Cross-Cultural Study of Beliefs in Out-of-the-Body Experiences, Waking and Sleeping." *Journal of the Society for Psychical Research,* March 1978.

Sheldrake, Rupert, "Is Death a Dream?" *The Unexplained* (London), Vol. 11, Issue 125.

Shenker, Israel, "Group Here to Begin Search for Evidence

of Human Soul." *New York Times,* July 29, 1971.

Shepard, Leslie, ed., *Encyclopedia of Occultism & Parapsychology.* Vol. 1. Detroit: Gale Research, 1984.

"She's Having the Time of Her Lives." *People,* January 26, 1987.

Smythe, J. Henry, Jr., comp. and ed., *The Amazing Benjamin Franklin.* New York: Frederick A. Stokes, 1929.

Stearn, Jess, *Edgar Cayce—The Sleeping Prophet.* New York: Bantam Books, 1967.

Stevenson, Ian:
"American Children Who Claim to Remember Previous Lives." *Journal of Nervous and Mental Disease,* Vol. 171, No. 12, 1983.
"Cryptomnesia and Parapsychology." *Journal of the Society for Psychical Research,* February 1983.
Cases of the Reincarnation Type, Vol. 2: Ten Cases in Sri Lanka. Charlottesville: University Press of Virginia, 1977.
Cases of the Reincarnation Type, Vol. 3: Twelve Cases in Lebanon and Turkey. Charlottesville: University Press of Virginia, 1980.
"The Evidence for Survival from Claimed Memories of Former Incarnations" (pamphlet). Originally published in the *Journal of the American Society for Psychical Research,* April-July 1960.
"Explanatory Value of the Idea of Reincarnation." *Journal of Nervous and Mental Disease,* Vol. 164, No. 5, 1977.
"The 'Perfect' Reincarnation Case." *Research in Parapsychology,* 1972.
"Reincarnation: Field Studies and Theoretical Issues." In

Handbook of Parapsychology, ed. by Benjamin B. Wolman. New York: Van Nostrand Reinhold, 1977.
"Research into the Evidence of Man's Survival after Death." *Journal of Nervous and Mental Disease,* Vol. 165, No. 3, 1977.
"Some Questions Related to Cases of the Reincarnation Type." *Journal of the American Society for Psychical Research,* October 1974.
Twenty Cases Suggestive of Reincarnation. Charlottesville: University Press of Virginia, 1974.
Xenoglossy. Charlottesville: University Press of Virginia, 1974.

Strayer, Joseph R., *The Albigensian Crusades.* New York: Dial Press, 1971.

Sugrue, Thomas, *There Is a River: The Story of Edgar Cayce.* Virginia Beach, Va.: A.R.E. Press, 1973.

Swann, Ingo, *To Kiss Earth Good-bye.* New York: Hawthorn Books, 1975.

Tansley, David V., *Subtle Body: Essence and Shadow.* New York: Thames and Hudson, 1977.

Thomas, Joseph, *Universal Pronouncing Dictionary of Biography and Mythology.* Philadelphia: J. B. Lippincott, 1930.

Turner, W. J., *Mozart: The Man & His Works.* New York: Alfred A. Knopf, 1938.

Valli, Éric, and Christine de Cherisey, *Tsangbou: Entre Népal et Tibet.* Neuchâtel, Switzerland, Hachette Realités, 1981.

Venn, Jonathan, "Hypnosis and the Reincarnation Hypothesis: A Critical Review and Intensive Case Study." *Jour-*

nal of the American Society for Psychical Research, October 1986.

Viereck, George Sylvester, "Henry Ford: Master Mind Sends Messages to Earth: An Interview with Henry Ford." *San Francisco Examiner,* August 26, 1928.

Walker, Benjamin, *Beyond the Body.* London: Routledge & Kegan Paul, 1974.

Wambach, Helen, *Reliving Past Lives: The Evidence under Hypnosis.* New York: Harper & Row, 1978.

Ward, Fred, "Long-Forbidden Tibet." *National Geographic,* February 1980.

Warrior: The Story of General George S. Patton, by the Editors of the *Army Times.* New York: G. P. Putnam's Sons, 1967.

Williams, Loring G., "Reincarnation of a Civil War Victim." *Fate,* December 1966.

Wilson, Colin, *Mysterious Powers.* Danbury, Conn.: Danbury Press, 1975.

Wilson, Ian:
All in the Mind. Garden City, N.Y.: Doubleday, 1982.
Mind out of Time? London: Victor Gollancz, 1981.

Woodhouse, Mark, "Near-Death Experiences and the Mind-Body Problem." *Anabiosis* (Storrs, Conn.), July 1981.

Wren, Christopher S., "Briton with a Sense of Déjà Vu Calls Ruins 'Home.' " *New York Times,* April 17, 1979.

Wurtman, Richard J., and Julius Axelrod, "The Pineal Gland." *Scientific American,* July 1965.

Zaleski, Carol, *Otherworld Journeys.* New York: Oxford University Press, 1987.

PICTURE CREDITS

The sources for the illustrations in this book are shown below. Credits from left to right are separated by semicolons, from top to bottom by dashes.

7: National Air and Space Museum, Smithsonian Institution; Hemingway Collection in the John F. Kennedy Library, Boston; National Archives Neg. No. 11-SC-17592. 8, 9: National Air and Space Museum, Smithsonian Institution; art by Donald Gates. 10, 11: Art by Donald Gates; Hemingway Collection in the John F. Kennedy Library, Boston. 12, 13: National Archives Neg. No. 11-SC-17592; art by Donald Gates. 15: Art by Kimmerle Milnazik. 16, 17: British Museum, London, © Michael Holford, London. 18, 19: C. M. Dixon/Photoresources, Canterbury, Kent; Camera Press, London; Mary Evans Picture Library, London; painting by G. W. Russell, courtesy the Hugh Lane Municipal Gallery of Modern Art, Dublin; *Flight of the Shaman* by Jessie Oonark, Baker Lake, Northwest Territories, Canada, reproduced with permission of the Estate of Jessie Oonark. Photo by Ernest P. Mayer, courtesy the Winnipeg Art Gallery, George Swinton Collection. 20: Mary Evans Picture Library, London/*Psychic News.* 21: Mary Evans Picture Library, London. 23 montage: Painting by Mihran K. Serailian, courtesy Manly P. Hall, Philosophical Research Society, Los Angeles, photographed by Werts Studios, Inc., silver cord by art studio. 24, 25: Silver cord by art studio. 26: Mary Evans Picture Library, London, silver cord by art studio. 28, 29: From *The Projection of the Astral Body,* by Sylvan J. Muldoon and Hereward Carrington, Rider & Co., London, 1929, except left, Mary Evans Picture Library, London. 30, 31: © 1987 David Michael Kennedy. 33-35: Duane Michals. 37: Drawing by

Susan Blackmore. 38, 39: Henry Groskinsky/TIME Magazine. 40: John Hartwell. 41: Mark Handler, photographer, from *Psi SEARCH, The New Investigation of Psychic Phenomena that Separates Fact from Speculation,* by Bowles and Hynds, Harper & Row, New York, 1978. 43: © Roger Ressmeyer/Wheeler Pictures. 45: Art by Wendy Popp, detail from pages 52, 53. 46-55: Art by Wendy Popp. 57: Art by Kimmerle Milnazik. 58: Hugh R. Downs. 61: Painting by Cristoforo Roncalli, courtesy S. Maria in Vallicella, Rome, photographed by Aldo Durazzi. 62, 63: BPCC/Aldus Archive, London. 64: Henry Groskinsky. 66: Photograph by Mal Warshaw from *To Live until We Say Good-Bye,* by Elisabeth Kübler-Ross, Prentice-Hall, Inc., 1978. 68: Detail of *Ascent to Purgatory* by Hieronymus Bosch, Palazzo Ducale, Venice, photo Scala, Florence. 70, 71: Pen and watercolor by Bryan Leister. 74, 75: Art by William Blake, courtesy the Trustees of the British Museum, London—from *Blake's Grave; a Prophetic Book,* edited by S. Foster Damon, Brown University Press, Providence, R.I., 1963, used with permission of University Press of New England, Hanover, N.H. 76: Watercolor by William Blake, courtesy the Trustees of the British Museum, London. 79: Art by Susi Kilgore, detail from pages 84, 85. 80-87: Art by Susi Kilgore. 89: John Senzer. 90, 91: Western History Collections, University of Oklahoma. 92, 93 photomontage: Background courtesy Arizona Historical Society, Tucson, face photographed by Steve Tuttle. 94, 95 photomontage: Background courtesy Library of Congress, body photographed by Steve Tuttle. 97: Art by Kimmerle Milnazik. 98, 99: Courtesy the Board of Trustees of the Victoria and Albert Museum, London, photo courtesy Photoresources, Canterbury, Kent. 100: Engraving by Émile Bayard,

Explorer Archives, collection Devaux, Paris. 101: From *We Are One Another* by Arthur Guirdham, © 1974, published by C. W. Daniels, Saffron Walden, Essex. 102, 103: Richard Riddell. 104, 105: Library of Congress. 107: Hanny M. El-Zeini, Cairo, except left, courtesy collection of M. Tracey, London. 110, 111: Hylton Edgar Hexham, courtesy Nancy Edgar, inset courtesy Syndication International, London. 113: AP/Wide World Photos. 115: John Beckett. 116: Orin Sealy for *Denver Post.* 117: © June 6, 1956, *Chicago American,* all rights reserved, used with permission of the *Chicago Tribune.* 118: J. Dixon-Scott, London—Culver Pictures, Inc. 119: © June 6, 1956, *Chicago American,* all rights reserved, used with permission of the *Chicago Tribune.* 120: Courtesy the Board of Trustees of the Victoria and Albert Museum, London. 121: Inset, Baldez/Shostal—*Yugoslav Review,* Belgrade. 122: BBC Hulton Picture Library, London—courtesy Musée Condé de Chantilly, France, photo Derek Bayes/Aspect Picture Library, London. 123: Library of Congress—painting by Philippe de Champaigne, collection U. Moussalli, Paris, photo Bulloz, Paris. 125: Suomen Kuvapalvelu Oy, Helsinki. 126: Trans. No. 2467 (photo by Lee Boltin), courtesy Department Library Services, American Museum of Natural History, New York. 128: © Marilyn Silverstone/Magnum, reprinted with permission of Aperture Foundation, Inc. 129: Gu Shoukang, Foreign Languages Press, Beijing, China. 130, 131: © Marilyn Silverstone/ Magnum, reprinted with permission of Aperture Foundation, Inc.; *Yugoslav Review,* Belgrade. 132, 133: *Yugoslav Review,* Belgrade; Lauren Stockbower. 134, 135: Eric Valli, Saint-Jorioz, France. 136, 137: *Yugoslav Review,* Belgrade.

INDEX

Time-Life Books Inc.
is a wholly owned subsidiary of
TIME INCORPORATED

FOUNDER: Henry R. Luce 1898-1967

Editor-in-Chief: Jason McManus
Chairman and Chief Executive Officer: J. Richard Munro
President and Chief Operating Officer: N. J. Nicholas, Jr.
Editorial Director: Ray Cave
Executive Vice President, Books: Kelso F. Sutton
Vice President, Books: George Artandi

TIME-LIFE BOOKS INC.

EDITOR: George Constable
Executive Editor: Ellen Phillips
Director of Design: Louis Klein
Director of Editorial Resources: Phyllis K. Wise
Editorial Board: Russell B. Adams, Jr., Dale M. Brown,
Roberta Conlan, Thomas H. Flaherty, Lee Hassig, Donia
Ann Steele, Rosalind Stubenberg, Kit van Tulleken,
Henry Woodhead
Director of Photography and Research:
John Conrad Weiser

PRESIDENT: Christopher T. Linen
Chief Operating Officer: John M. Fahey, Jr.
Senior Vice President: James L. Mercer
Vice Presidents: Stephen L. Bair, Ralph J. Cuomo, Neal
Goff, Stephen L. Goldstein, Juanita T. James, Hallett
Johnson III, Carol Kaplan, Susan J. Maruyama, Robert H.
Smith, Paul R. Stewart, Joseph J. Ward
Director of Production Services: Robert J. Passantino

Editorial Operations
Copy Chief: Diane Ullius
Production: Celia Beattie
Quality Control: James J. Cox (director)
Library: Louise D. Forstall

MYSTERIES OF THE UNKNOWN

SERIES DIRECTOR: Russell B. Adams, Jr.
Series Administrator: Elise Ritter Gibson
Designer: Herbert H. Quarmby

Editorial Staff for *Psychic Voyages*
Associate Editors: Jane N. Coughran (pictures);
Pat Daniels (text)
Writers: Janet P. Cave, Laura Foreman
Assistant Designer: Lorraine D. Rivard
Copy Coordinator: Darcie Conner Johnston
Picture Coordinator: Betty H. Weatherly
Editorial Assistant: Donna Fountain

Special Contributors: Christine Hinze (London, picture
research); George Daniels, Donald Jackson, Wendy
Murphy, Marilynne R. Rudick, John Tompkins, Robert H.
White (text); Eleanor Barrett, John Drummond, Ellen
Robling (design); Richard A. Davis (research)

Correspondents: Elisabeth Kraemer-Singh (Bonn); Maria
Vincenza Aloisi (Paris); Ann Natanson (Rome).
Valuable assistance was also provided by Jaime A.
Florcruz, Jane Zhang, Zhen Zhang (Beijing); Pavle Svabic
(Belgrade); Mona Mortagy (Cairo); Lance Keyworth
(Helsinki); Bing Wong (Hong Kong); Judy Aspinall
(London); Elizabeth Brown, Christina Lieberman (New
York); Dag Christensen (Oslo); Ann Wise (Rome); Phillip
Cunningham (Shanghai).

The research for *Psychic Voyages* was prepared under the
supervision of Time-Life Books by:
Bibliographics Inc.
President: David L. Harrison
Researchers: Vilasini Balakrishnian, Mary Ford Dreesen,
Martha L. Johnson, Sydney Johnson, Mary Mayberry, Jared
Rosenfeld, Jacqueline Shaffer, Corinne Szabo

The Consultants:
Marcello Truzzi, professor of sociology at Eastern
Michigan University, is also director of the Center for
Scientific Anomalies Research (CSAR) and editor of its
journal, the *Zetetic Scholar.* Dr. Truzzi, who considers
himself a "constructive skeptic" with regard to claims of
the paranormal, works through the CSAR to produce
dialogues between critics and proponents of unusual
scientific claims.

James G. Matlock is librarian and archivist of the
American Society for Psychical Research (ASPR). He is a
member of the Parapsychological Association and has
written extensively on the history of parapsychology and
reincarnation.

Other Publications:

TIME FRAME
FIX IT YOURSELF
FITNESS, HEALTH & NUTRITION
SUCCESSFUL PARENTING
HEALTHY HOME COOKING
UNDERSTANDING COMPUTERS
LIBRARY OF NATIONS
THE ENCHANTED WORLD
THE KODAK LIBRARY OF CREATIVE PHOTOGRAPHY
GREAT MEALS IN MINUTES
THE CIVIL WAR
PLANET EARTH
COLLECTOR'S LIBRARY OF THE CIVIL WAR
THE EPIC OF FLIGHT
THE GOOD COOK
WORLD WAR II
HOME REPAIR AND IMPROVEMENT
THE OLD WEST

*For information on and a full description of any of the
Time-Life Books series listed above, please call 1-800-621-
7026, or write:*
Reader Information
Time-Life Customer Service
P.O. Box C-32068
Richmond, Virginia 23261-2068

This volume is one of a series that examines the history
and nature of seemingly paranormal phenomena. Other
books in the series include:
Mystic Places
Psychic Powers
The UFO Phenomenon

Library of Congress Cataloging in Publication Data
Psychic voyages.
  (Mysteries of the unknown).
  Bibliography: p.
  Includes index.
  1. Near-death experiences.
I. Time-Life Books. II. Series.
BF1045.N4P78 1988   133.9'01'3   87-18126
ISBN 0-8094-6316-4
ISBN 0-8094-6317-2 (lib. bdg.)